DATE DUE

~~JE 1 1 01~~			
~~NO 6 01~~			
~~Ap~~			
~~MY 2 2 03~~			
~~JE 1 1 03~~			
~~JE 2 04~~			
~~JE 2 4 14~~			
DE 3 19			

GARLAND STUDIES IN

AMERICAN POPULAR HISTORY AND CULTURE

edited by

JEROME NADELHAFT
UNIVERSITY OF MAINE

A GARLAND SERIES

CHICANO IMAGES

REFIGURING ETHNICITY
IN MAINSTREAM FILM

CHRISTINE LIST

GARLAND PUBLISHING, INC.
NEW YORK & LONDON / 1996

Library of Congress Cataloging-in-Publication Data

List, Christine.
    Chicano images : refiguring ethnicity in mainstream film /
Christine List.
        p.   cm. — (Garland studies in American popular history
and culture)
        Includes bibliographical references (p.   ) and index.
        ISBN 0-8153-2060-4 (alk. paper)
        1. Mexican Americans in motion pictures.   I. Title.
II. Series.
PN1995.9.M49L57 1996
791.43'652036872073—dc20

                                                    95-53204

Printed on acid-free, 250-year-life paper
Manufactured in the United States of America

For Michael, Payton, and Nora

CONTENTS

Chicano Images

I

INTRODUCTION: CONTEXTS OF CHICANO FEATURE FILMMAKING

> To call oneself Chicano is an overt political act.
>
> —Santos Martinez Jr.[1]

The Chicano Movement began as a grassroots nationalist call for Mexican American unity in the 1960s. By the late 1970s, the Movement had become more mainstream, carrying out most of its activities through Democratic Party politics, social service organizations and Chicano Studies programs.[2] In the area of cinema, a similar mainstreaming occurred which resulted in the expansion of Chicano filmmaking beyond short format experimental and documentary pieces into the arena of the narrative feature. The feature format offered certain advantages for filmmakers who saw themselves as part of the Chicano Cultural Movement; the opportunity to transmit a cultural message through a highly entertaining mass medium and the possibility of reaching ethnically diverse North American audiences with an image that could counter Hollywood stereotypes.

Yet the strategic cultural/political benefits of the feature format were counterbalanced by certain negative factors connected with the Hollywood formulas incorporated into the films. The restrictive structural aspects of the narrative feature presented many aesthetic and ideological problems, especially in terms of how the narrative conventions conveyed ethnic identity. Realizing this, many Chicano filmmakers developed ways of refiguring narrative conventions to construct new representations of Chicano culture. This study examines these techniques and offers an explanation of how such self-representational strategies shape the construction of Chicano and Chicana identity.

THE CHICANO CULTURAL MOVEMENT

To better understand the films in this study as manifestations of *Chicanismo* and an "ethnic" cinema movement, it is useful to briefly look at the cultural history behind the Chicano Movement. In their classic study of Chicano Art, Tomás Ybarra-Frausto and Shifra Goldman periodize Chicano history into four different eras.[3] They mark the first historical epoch between the years 1598 and 1821. Over the course of these two centuries the Spanish colonizers moved north from central Mexico into what is now the southwestern United States. Once in the north, the Spanish intermarried with the existing Indian populations. Over the next two hundred years, there was a fruitful process of cultural exchange between the Spanish and Indian artisans which was reflected in the architecture, pottery, weaving and other arts.

The second period in the history of Chicano culture dates from 1821 to 1910, from the establishment of Mexico as an independent nation to the beginnings of the Mexican Revolution. During this time the great distance between Mexico City and the northern frontier meant that the northern territory (the region which became the Southwestern United States) was largely ignored by the Mexican government. This physical and political distance from the capital led to secessionist ideas in the north. The independent status of the area also invigorated local artistic production in the borderlands.[4] Farther west, in southern California, an abusive discriminatory system of peonage which was first introduced through the missions and continued by a small group of wealthy landowners, kept Indians and lower class *mestizos* (people of mixed blood) in virtual servitude. This system was supplanted by massive immigration of Anglos from the east who instigated what was essentially a second conquest of the region. In 1848, after a war that led to the signing of the Treaty of Guadalupe Hidalgo, Mexico was forced to give away her northern provinces which made up approximately one third of the country's overall lands. The conquered territory now comprises the states of California, Colorado, Utah, Texas, Arizona, Nevada and New Mexico in the United States.

Continued Anglo penetration of the Southwest during this era was facilitated by the building of the railways. The influx led to a brutal marginalization and suppression of Mexican culture in the U.S. Widespread racial oppression forced a decline in the Mexican American visual arts which had been previously supported by the Mexican elite. The folk arts, however, managed to sustain themselves during the Anglo invasion and, in fact, flourished. Some of the traditional arts which survived were artifacts of Catholicism, such as home altars and funerary decorations, along with crafts constructed for fiestas.

The third period in Chicano history is termed "The Mexican American Period" (1910-1965). It began with the Mexican Revolution (1910-1917) which, coupled with the economic exploitation by US corporations in Mexico, triggered one of the largest displacements of a population in history. Millions of Mexicans migrated north.[5] Many settled in the *barrios* of the Southwest. Others migrated to Chicago and the industrialized cities of the Midwest. It was during this period that artists, photographers and artisans came north from Mexico. Some of the most influential work of this era was produced by the great Mexican muralists José Clemente Orozco, Diego Rivera and David Alfaro Siqueros.

Chicanos also generated vibrant manifestations of their own culture during this period, most notably, the formation of a *pachuco* subculture in the 1940's. *Pachuquismo* was at once a synthesis and rejection of Anglo American and Mexican culture. The *pachucos* and *pachucas* were Mexican American adolescents who formed a counter-culture in response to the alienation and marginalization they felt in the U.S. With their zoot suit style of clothing and their own dialect of Spanish and English called *caló*, the *pachuco* culture expressed a public rebelliousness toward both Anglo and Mexican traditions. In the art of this period, the *pachuco* culture quickly became mythologized. Over time, several Chicano artists elevated the *pachuco* to the status of Chicano anti-hero and transformed him into a cultural icon.

Goldman and Ybarra-Frausto describe the more recent decades of Chicano history as "The Chicano Period." They break this period down into two subcategories. The first begins in 1965 with the Farm Workers' struggle and ends in the mid-seventies at a point when many of the Chicano activist organizations disbanded. The second period follows from the mid-seventies to the present. The initial years of the first period were typified by the existence of noncommercial, community oriented groups of artists and activists who set up cultural collectives across the U.S. Their various cultural products were infused with a sense of political immediacy. Cultural nationalism and separatism informed much of their art. The nationalist philosophy which grounded the Movement was fueled by the popularization of the concept of Aztlán, the name of the mythical homeland of the Chicano people. Aztlán symbolized an indigenous paradise lost in the Southwest; the land of the ancestors. The myth of Aztlán served as a crucial master narrative for the Movement, and from it sprang a wealth of Chicano art.

The United Farm Workers, under the leadership of César Chávez was also a pivotal organization during the Chicano period. The Farm Workers Movement provided the most enduring visual symbols of this era. The Virgin of Guadalupe and the red, black and white thunderbird flag became indelible images of Chicanismo. The Farm Workers' struggle also gave birth to the Teatro Campesino, an agit-prop theatre company which Luis Valdez developed to carry out the goals of the union through the creation of a cultural front. The Teatro Campesino became a site of immense creativity and played a major role in fomenting the Cultural Movement as a whole.

Also during the first Chicano period, Chicano political parties, most importantly the La Raza Unida Party, were formed. The political groups sought major changes in local politics. Other Chicano political organizations included a vigorous student movement which was organized at local and national levels. It was the student movement that was responsible for the famous East Los Angeles High School "blowouts" where thousands of Chicano students walked out in 1969 demanding an end to discriminatory treatment.

The art and political thinking of this Chicano decade developed hand in hand with other cultural and political movements of the sixties. Black Power, with its cultural nationalist roots, community organizing and highly visible self-defense groups, provided a model for Chicano nationalists and their "Brown Power"/"Raza Power" militant stance.[6] The Cuban Revolution also lent inspiration to El Movimiento, influencing Chicanos to include Third World issues and anti-imperialist demands to their agenda. The Anti-Vietnam War Movement also drew thousands of Chicanos to public protests. During one such protest in East Los Angeles in August 1970 police attacked demonstrators and killed two Chicanos. One of those killed was Rubén Salazar, a journalist with the *Los Angeles Times*. The victims were remembered in murals, posters, paintings and documentary films.

At the same time the anti-war movement was inspiring Chicanos to embrace tactics of civil disobedience, the American Indian Movement (AIM) was pressuring the U.S. government for return of native lands and demanding restitution for the numerous abuses of treaty rights. Though unsuccessful in obtaining their goals, AIM received national media visibility. Their activities inspired a Chicano group organized by Reies Lopéz Tijerina to take over public lands in New Mexico. Tijerina maintained that the lands had been granted to the Chicano people as part of the Treaty of Guadalupe Hidalgo. Tijerina drew upon the notion of indigenous Chicano homelands (Aztlán) to strengthen popular support for the issue of Chicano land rights. His struggle appealed to the sense of neo-indigenism and the quest for social justice that formed the ideological platform for the Movement.

Feminism also played a significant role in forming the Chicano consciousness of that period. Goldman and Ybarra-Frausto point out that Chicana artists were very much influenced by Frida Kahlo and her aggressive, independent approach to cultural production. Women's collectives, such as Mujeres Artistas del Suroeste, were active during this time. The role of women cultural workers in the Movement underwent many challenges and was ultimately strengthened.

Another formative social movement at that time was the highly publicized prisoners' rights campaign. The highly publicized "Soledad Brothers" incident and the FBI's persistent jailing of Black Panthers were events which drew national attention to imprisonment as a means of political control of minority populations. In the U.S., Chicano prisoners (called *pintos* in *caló*) were disproportionately incarcerated compared to the Anglo population. Chicano inmates organized and sent their agenda back to the *barrios* by writing poetry and publishing newspapers. Their predicament became a dominant theme in Chicano Art and a metaphor for imprisonment of Chicanos in the *barrios* and *colonias* of the United States.

The art produced during these formative years of the Movement tended to be based on alternative cultural models. The key organizing concepts of the 1960's—*recuerdo* (memory), *descubrimiento* (discovery) and *voluntad* (affirmation)—reflected the influence of Chicano novelist Tomás Rivera on Chicano artists.[7] The three terms emphasized the need for the resurrection and foregrounding of traditional cultural practices to construct a *Chicanismo* which could mobilize the masses around a new nationalist identity. To meet these goals, vernacular forms of artistic expression were developed which were popular with the largely working class and underclass audiences. It was the close relationship to their audience which inspired Chicano and Chicana cultural producers to develop Chicano art as a politically committed cultural form.

In the mid-1970s, there was a decline in ethnic nationalism. New forms of artistic expression began to emerge giving way to more individual experimentation. By the 1980s, basic assumptions of Chicano and Chicana identity which had informed earlier work came under scrutiny. *Chicanismo* became increasingly defined by its diversity. A multifaceted view of identity which included factors of social class, sexual preference, gender, regional culture and ethnic influences, among others, provided a competing and alternative interpretation to the fixed nationalist model of *Chicanismo*. Chicano artists actively embraced a multicultural paradigm which had been popularized by the Border Arts Workshop in California. This meant that Chicano and Chicana artists increasingly saw themselves as part of an international movement of progressive artists and their art as evidence of a constantly shifting notion of *Chicanismo*.

In the nineties, it is common for Chicanos to call themselves by something other than Chicano. In certain instances Chicanos will use terms like Hispanic or Latino/a as self-identifying labels. Director Luis Valdez has elected to use the terms Hispanic and Latino under certain circumstances to legitimize his own *mestizaje* and to call attention to the Mexican elements in the larger multiracial culture that he sees as the new defining identity in the U.S.[8] Valdez's stance is a call to mobilize diversity. This call is taking on a new urgency as anti-immigrant sentiments within the Anglo population surface around the issue of California Proposition 187 (a measure which would severely cut government services for immigrants). In the nineties, thousands of Hispanics are coming together across the country to protest against the growing white backlash. As a result Chicanos, Puerto Ricans, Central Americans and others are building coalitions which erase nationalist ethnic lines. This move is reflective of the political exigencies of our time and serves to bridge *Chicanismo* with other movements and peoples with similar progressive agendas.

INSTITUTIONAL CONTEXTS OF
CHICANO FILM PRODUCTION

Chicano participation in the Hollywood mainstream has always been limited by a pervasive racism which plagues the industry. Although during the first decades of the twentieth century there were a number of major stars of Mexican American descent, the roles they played were significantly restricted and stereotyped. Other areas of the industry employed Chicanos as technicians and talent agents, but in the field of directing Chicano talent went untapped. To date we have documented the existence of only one Chicano feature director producing before the 1960s. He was Eustacio Montoya, an independent filmmaker who shot, produced and exhibited his films in the 1910s and 1920s. Archivists refused to preserve his work and, as a result the prints of his films have deteriorated to the point where only a few still frames remain.[9]

It wasn't until the late 1960s that the first body of Chicano directed films began to appear. In 1966, Ernie Palomino directed a short called *My Trip in a '52 Ford*. In 1969, Luis Valdez of Teatro Campesino made a short documentary, *I am Joaquin,* illustrating a popular poem of Chicano nationalism. At the same time the Chicano Film Movement was emerging, a strong community protest effort was being launched against television stations demanding real access for Chicanos to the means of production.[10] The first media outlets to respond and open their doors to Chicanos were local television stations in the southwest,[11] particularly in the Los Angeles area.[12] As a result, a number of talk show format television programs were produced by Chicanos in the early seventies.[13] In addition to the community service/events programs, KCET-TV in Los Angeles also funded a show called *Canción de la raza* (Song of My People), a family melodrama dealing with experiences of the Chicano community. Sixty-five episodes aired between 1968 and 1970. Eduardo Moreno was responsible for many of the productions in this series.[14]

During this same time frame, community training programs run by local stations and Los Angeles area universities began to teach filmmaking to interested Chicanos. This spawned a generation of filmmakers including Susan Racho (*Garment Workers in Southern California*, 1975), Sylvia Morales (*Chicana*, 1979), José Luis Ruiz (*Los Vendidos*, 1972) and Moctesuma Esparza, the producer of *Only Once in a Lifetime* (1978) and *Milagro Beanfield War* (1988). Esparza's master's thesis, *Cinco Vidas* (1972), a study of a five Chicano individuals living in East Los Angeles, was backed by KNBC and won him an Emmy for best documentary in 1974.

While the support of local television stations offered an outlet for Chicano film and video producers, the nature of the support presented many creative limitations for the producers. Minuscule production budgets were a crucial factor in forcing Chicano producers to find inexpensive ways to express themselves.[15] A number of strategies were developed to circumvent the economic and artistic restraints placed upon the Chicano television shows. For example Treviño's series, *Acción Chicano*, which aired on KCET-TV in 1972, combined its own funding resources with the budget from a Puerto Rican series called *Realidades*. As a result the producers of both series were able to shoot five episodes which they then exchanged among themselves for broadcast. According to Chon Noriega, the documentaries produced for the series, "subverted the objective discourse of reportage in order to pioneer a new form of television, the political documentary series, which protested the Vietnam War, advocated a farmworkers' union, and exposed the racism of the criminal legal system."[16] Such low budget coping strategies developed during the formative years of Chicano filmmaking would be carried over to feature filmmaking as the filmmakers would, again be faced with extremely limited production budgets.

In 1974, Chicanos combined forces with other Latino producers to form the Latino Consortium. Based at KCET-TV, the Consortium consisted of ten stations that shared tapes by and about Latinos. In 1979, the Latino Consortium received support from the Corporation for Public Broadcasting to set up a distribution network. Through the efforts of the consortium, member stations agreed to give money for twenty-six half-hour shows to be produced. The Latino Consortium eventually changed its name to the National Latino Communications Center and is still actively promoting work by Latino directors.

Another influential event in the evolution of Chicano film was initiated in 1975 when *Realidades* was picked up by the Public Broadcasting System and became the first national Latino television series. In the two years the series ran, it received $553,687 from the Corporation for Public Broadcasting (CPB) to produce a total of twenty-three half-hour programs. However, that sum was only approximately three percent of the total funds CPB allocated for productions.[17] Chicano producers decided to confront this crisis in funding and formed their own lobbying group, the National Latino Media Coalition. It was the efforts of the Coalition, to secure public television and national endowment funds which led to governmental support of Chicano feature films in the eighties.[18] Many important Chicano features were supported with federal dollars. Luis Valdez was the recipient of an National Endowment for the Arts grant to research the zoot suit riots for the play which eventually became the film *Zoot Suit* (1981). The producers of *El Norte* (1985), Gregory Nava and Ana Thomas, were awarded CPB funds for the film they made for the American Playhouse series. In the nineties, federal money remains a critical source of funds for the production and distribution of Chicano films. *The Devil Never Sleeps* (1994) and *. . . and the earth did not swallow him* (1994) received support from the National Endowment for the Arts and the ITVS.

As Chicano filmmakers have become more involved in feature productions, they have moved far beyond the budgets of public television to an economic arena where much more pressure is placed on the director/producer to produce films for profit. Securing financing from Hollywood investors for Chicano features has been difficult. Profitability for Chicano films is often predicated on the film's perceived ability to "cross over" to other markets. Chicano filmmakers have suffered the racial bias of Hollywood financiers who regard investing in Chicano productions as an unprecedented risk.

Hollywood seemed prepared to promote a "Latino Boom" in the eighties, but statistical data shows that there was relatively little participation by Hispanics. The number of Latinos and Latinas in the film industry has remained at nearly the same level despite more than a 100 percent increase in the U.S. Latino population. From 1970 to 1990 the Latino population grew from 9.1 million to over 20 million, with Latinos representing about 10% of the total U.S. population. In a report released in 1992 by the Director's Guild of America the number of days worked by Hispanic directors in film and television projects was only 1.3% of the days worked by its total membership.[19] It should be mentioned that over the past decade, Hollywood has made weak attempts to remedy its inequalities. Several studios set up minority internships in screenwriting and assistant directing. Universal sponsored a writing competition for Hispanic screenwriters which gave limited entry to the winners. Unfortunately, participation in these programs did not translate into feature directing opportunities for Chicanos.

Despite the scarcity of funds for Chicano features, Chicano directors were not afraid to challenge the system and produce films according to their own vision. As a cinema movement, their films posed a clear alternative to the mainstream, and early on they articulated a confrontational position towards Hollywood. In 1978, a group of Chicano directors banded together to form the Chicano Cinema Coalition. Their purpose was to define the aesthetic and ideological parameters of what they saw as a Chicano Cinema Movement. Sometimes meeting in director's Jesús Treviño's living room, they screened "classic" Hollywood narratives and debated the merits of the Hollywood form as a tool for establishing a progressive Chicano cinema.

> A Chicano alternative cinema ideology and philosophy which stresses the use of film and videotape for the decolonization, independence, advancement, *concientizacion* and national liberation of the Mexican and Chicano people in the United States . . . [20]

The aesthetic orientation of the Chicano Cinema Coalition and the Chicano film Movement was informed by Latin American theories of alternative and oppositional cinema. This influence is especially evident in an early manifesto by San Francisco based Chicano media critic Francisco X. Camplís:

> Rocha warns that Hollywood is dangerous for us, but so is Sartre. I feel that our search for ideas and models which help us to develop our own Raza cinema does not end with Rocha, Solanas, et. al. But their inspiration and motivation has given us a certain . . . sense of direction.[21]

The coupling of their acknowledgement of Latin American as well as European progressive influences with a sense of cautious hesitation towards these same theories signaled the preoccupation of Chicano filmmakers with their own nationalist agenda. But the earlier manifestations of nationalism eventually gave way to a more ample articulation of a multicultural filmmaking practice. Chicano filmmaking encompasses hundreds of individual films and videos of many modes and genres of filmmaking. As a body of work, Chicano film can be characterized as a cinema of affirmation and resistance; affirming Chicano culture while resisting regressive hegemonic forces that circumscribe Chicano and Chicana self-expression.[22]

Chicano features have reached their audience through a number of different venues. Many of the films have received theatrical release. These include, *Born in East L.A.*(1987), *American Me* (1992), *Milagro Beanfield War* (1988), *El Mariachi* (1992), *Only Once in a Lifetime* (1978), *El Norte* (1985), *Heart Breaker* (1983), *Break of Dawn* (1988), *Zoot Suit* (1981), *La Bamba* (1987), *Raíces de sangre* (1977), *My Family* (1994) and the Cheech and Chong comedy films. Other films such as *Cisco Kid* (1994) by Luis Valdez received a commercial television release. Severo Perez's film . . . *and the earth did not swallow him* (1994) played on PBS. A number of Chicano feature directors such as Robert Díaz LeRoy (*River Bottom*, 1993), Juan Frausto *(Change*, 1994) and Frank Perry López *(Last Train Out*, 1993) have found audiences by tapping into the film festival and university distribution circuits or through foreign distribution. As a body of work reaching millions of viewers, Chicano features provide a public forum for Chicano cultural expression and articulate issues of Chicano identity on a national and international scale.

ETHNIC REPRESENTATION AND IDENTITY POLITICS

Kobena Mercer has pointed out that ethnic identity as a cultural category has been manipulated for the purposes of the New Right as well as the New Left. He cautions that there is no progressive "essence" in an ethnic identity as such. Therefore, he concludes that it is important to historicize the question of cultural identity in contemporary cultural politics. This holds true for ethnic film culture as well.

Apart from Fanon's *The Wretched of the Earth* and *Black Skin, White Masks*, one of the most influential works on ethnic identity and cultural politics has been Edward Said's *Orientalism*. The book provides an in depth analysis of how the West reinterpreted Eastern cultures within a dominant paradigm of "otherness." Said outlines the cultural and political implications of this Western project as follows:

> One ought to remember that all cultures impose corrections upon raw reality, changing it from free-floating objects into units of knowledge. The problem is not that conversion takes place. It is perfectly natural for the human mind to resist the assault on it of untreated strangeness; therefore cultures have always been inclined to impose complete transformations on other cultures, receiving those other cultures not as they are but as, for the benefit of the receiver, they ought to be. To the Westerner, however, the Oriental was always like some aspect of the West . . . Yet the Orientalist makes it his work to be always converting the Orient from something into something else: he does this for himself, for the sake of his culture, in some cases for what he believes is the sake of the Oriental.[23]

Said offers us a cogent explanation of what happens when a dominant culture represents what it does not understand. His works speak to the problems inherent in imperialist representations of minion cultures. Representation of this sort rarely remains free of exploitation, coding the other according to the needs of the West.

The work of Homi Bhabha provides a deconstructionist method of analyzing Western images of Third World peoples by uncovering the processes of subjectification made possible through stereotypical discourse. Pointing out that Said fails to address the problem of ambivalence in Western representations of the Third World, Bhabha refashions a theory of colonialist representation of difference:

> . . . it gives access to an identity which is predicated as much on mastery and pleasure as it is on anxiety and defence, for it is a form of multiple and contradictory belief in its recognition of difference and disavowal of it.[24]

In other words, Bhabha contends that imperialism constructs images of the ethnic other which are not altogether negative, but more accurately explained as ambivalent. The ethnic other is often fetishized and held up as a bearer of what the imperialist is not supposed to desire, yet secretly covets. A love/hate relationship between First World and Third World is concretized through these stereotypes.

Related to Bhabha's notion of structured ambivalence, Robert Stam offers a view of cross-cultural representation which orients the direction of ethnic film studies towards a more dialectic approach. Stam's theory reworks Bakhtin's notions of polyglossia and dialogism. Bakhtin's method rests upon the idea that different voices can be combined to construct an identity with full resonances and perspectives about and of an ethnic group. As Stam transposes this theory on to ethnic film studies, the question of ethnic representation shifts from one of pluralism to "one of multi-vocality, an approach which would strive to abolish social inequalities while heightening and even cultivating cultural difference."[25] Stam proposes that "entire genres, languages and cultures" are susceptible to "mutual illumination" and therefore encourages scholars to study ethnicity in the cinema in comparative terms. By following Stam and juxtaposing systems of ethnic representations against themselves the problem of authentication is lessened. The focus of the cinematic investigation is shifted from "Is this real?" to "What does this tell us about the way an ethnic group is perceived by itself and by others?" Stam's approach has implications for this study. The focus of the analysis is not to judge whether or not Chicanos show their culture in a more realistic way than Hollywood. Instead, the investigation concentrates on the process of representation in Chicano films for the purpose of determining which variations in Chicano and Chicana ethnic identities are advanced by the text and by what means.

References to authenticity frequently enter into the discussion of ethnic representation and identity interpretation. Gayatri Spivak has remarked that she has been called upon many times to represent "the third world viewpoint."[26] Her single voice is sought by whites as emblematic of the category she is invited to champion, be it Indian women, immigrants, or the entire Third World. She points out that this type of positioning of ethnicity and the ethnic as a monolithic voice is endemic to the western view of ethnicity as inherent essence and is symptomatic of the colonialist impulse to deny the subjecthood of Third World peoples. Her insights serve as a basis for this study of Chicano Cinema as well. There is no assumption made that one authentic Chicano or Chicana film exists but rather a range of competing films which position Chicano and Chicana identity from various and often conflicting perspectives. This study will look at which identities are

privileged and which are absent or suppressed. In some cases, I will
shown that the ethnic director has, himself, bought into the notion of
the authentic by romanticizing his own view of *Chicanismo*.

The relentless impulse on the part of post-colonialist filmmakers to
depict "authenticity" is a recurrent issue in cultural studies. Stuart Hall
stresses the complexity posed by the project of self-representation for
the post-colonial Afro-Caribbean subject. He notes that because he/she
is self-inscribed with the "ambivalent identifications of the racist
world," (a phrase which Hall has taken from Homi Bhabha's
introduction to *The Wretched of the Earth*) "the dialogue of power and
resistance, of refusal and recognition, with and against 'Presence
Europenne' is almost as complex as the so-called 'dialogue' with
Africa."[27] Because of this, Hall asserts that instead of looking for
"one true identity," identity must be formulated as a "matter of
becoming as well as of being."

> It belongs to the future as much as to the past. It is not
> something which already exists, transcending place, time,
> history and culture. Cultural identities come from
> somewhere, have histories. But, like everything which is
> historical, they undergo constant transformation. Far from
> being eternally fixed in some essentialized past, they are
> subject to the continuous play of history, culture and
> power. Far from being grounded in a mere recovery of the
> past, which is waiting to be found, and which when found,
> will secure our sense of ourselves into eternity, identities
> are the names we give to the different ways we are
> positioned by and position ourselves within, the narratives
> of the past.[28]

Chicano culture has gone through a similar period of essentializing
Chicano identity. Much of this manifested itself through Chicano
nationalism. But as the Chicano Movement became more inclusive and
internationalized, the identity politics became increasingly more
malleable. Chicano artists and filmmakers began to construct identity
as transformative and represented Chicano ethnicity against the
complexities of the past and the ambiguity of the present. In Chicano
films the border region began to serve as a metaphor for identity in
transition, an identity rooted in conquest, migration and bi-cultural
power shifts. As artist Guillermo Gómez-Peña explains:

> When I'm asked about my nationality or ethnic identity, I
> can't give a one word answer, since my identity now has
> multiple repertoires: I'm Mexican, but also Chicano and
> Latin American. On the border they call me *chilango* or
> *mexquillo*; in Mexico City I'm a *pocho* or *norteño*; and in
> Europe I'm a *sudaca*. Anglos call me "Hispanic" or
> "Latino," and Germans have at times taken me for a Turk
> or an Italian.[29]

This understanding of the Chicano self as an identity in process yet
historically specific has lead to the production of Chicano films that go
beyond simply correcting an "inauthentic" depiction of *Chicanismo*.
Recent productions such as *The Devil Never Sleeps* and *Change* explore
and undermine assumptions of identity in Chicano culture. These films
create a dialogue on Chicano self-representation which transgresses
borders set up not only by Hollywood but by Chicano filmmakers
themselves.

FEATURE FILMMAKING IN CONTEXT

Chicano feature films are situated in a social/artistic matrix
that foregrounds important questions about the relationship between
ethnicity and activist cinema. The films interrogate the interplay
between the construction of a self image and the shaping forces of
mainstream popular culture. Because Chicano feature filmmakers take
from both the Hollywood apparatus and the cultural/political heritage
of the Chicano Movement, their work occupies a relatively unique
position in American culture (not unlike African American Cinema),
constituting a fertile laboratory for investigation of contemporary
theoretical concerns.

The economics of feature film production presents its own set of
problems for Chicano directors. Many lending institutions will often
refuse to advance independents money for a film unless the movie is
already under contract with a major distributor. Distributors often
demand certain assurances from the filmmakers such as guaranteeing
the use of stars or of well tested formula stories. In the eighties,
additional pressure was placed on directors when Hollywood revived
its "big budget production" approach to movie making. As Randall
Miller has pointed out, as far as the industry is concerned, it is much

easier to make a profitable large budget movie than a profitable small budget one.[30] This attitude may be rethought as young independents such a Quentin Tarantino (*Pulp Fiction*) and Robert Rodriquez (*Desperado*) prove that low budget films can bring in handsome profits. But the prevailing logic is still in favor of the blockbuster because a big budget movie is normally guaranteed an ample promotional budget by the studios due to the fact they have already put large sums of money into the film during the production phase. A strong advertising campaign, though not always a guarantee of success, has a significant impact on box office receipts. Directors of color are especially susceptible to ruin by promotional decisions beyond their control because they are frequently not part of Hollywood marketing departments. The marketing departments of the studios want to target "big grossers" to a national audience which, as Randall Miller explains, "necessarily implies dilutions of minority viewpoints in production and content."[31] People of color are also at a disadvantage because they generally work with lower budgeted films and because their aesthetic is frequently interpreted by whites as appealing to a select audience other than that which the director originally intended for the film.[32] Hence, the filmmaker of color is pressured to work on increasingly grander scales in order to acquire more profitability and control over his or her work.

Rosa Linda Fregoso has criticized the emphasis on "bigness" which plagues the film industry, calling it an example of the phallocentric power wielded within the patriarchal system of film production.[33] In opposition to the "35 mm" standard of achievement, Chicana filmmakers, she says, have consciously chosen to steer clear of feature film production, electing to work in the smaller format, lower budget modes of filmmaking. Of course, there is no way to substantiate the notion that Chicana filmmakers would not work in the mainstream feature format if given the opportunity. Nevertheless, the fact remains that Chicana filmmakers have been conspicuously absent in feature film productions, leaving the major creative decisions involving Chicano features under the control of Chicanos.

Hollywood as a controlling aesthetic and economic influence in the United States is a powerful institution Chicano directors must continually reckon with. The U.S. film industry has consistently proven its power to absorb oppositional styles. In *Classical Hollywood Cinema* Bordwell, Staiger and Thompson show how the distinctive nationalist film practices of Germany (Expressionism) and the Soviet Union (Montage) were emptied of their radical potential when Hollywood incorporated them into its the visual lexicon.[34] Pamela Falkenberg has commented on the ability of Hollywood to recuperate oppositional aesthetic practices of the European Art Cinema into mainstream film production.[35] Chicano Art Historians Shifra Goldman and Tomás Ybarra-Frausto aptly quote the following passage from Todd Gitlin's book, *The Whole World is Watching: Mass Media in the Making and Unmaking of the New Left* as commentary on the problematic relationship between oppositional and dominant cultures in the United States:

> In a floodlit society, it becomes extremely difficult, perhaps unimaginable, for an opposition movement to define itself and its world view, to build up an infrastructure of self-generated cultural institutions, outside the dominant culture.[36]

Early Chicano film manifestos and theoretical writings on Chicano film located Chicano narrative cinema outside the Hollywood paradigm placing it instead within a framework of popular culture developed by Latin American intellectuals known as *lo popular*. At the opposite end of the spectrum from mass culture, *lo popular* or popular culture was conceived as culture which expressed the voice of oppressed peoples by encouraging subaltern groups to speak for themselves through representation of their own popular practices.[37] A cinema which recovered the popular would resurrect a national consciousness and produce a social transformation.

But this oversimplified theory of resistance culture has been reevaluated by Jesús Martín-Barbero who asserts that such an understanding of *lo popular* as purely oppositional is reductionistic. Its proponents, he says, fail to understand popular culture as part of a cultural dynamic within transnational capitalism. The old theory of the popular does not account for the growing urbanization and intermingling of vernacular culture in Latin America. According to Martín-Barbero, cultural theorists should pay closer attention to the dynamic of popular resistance:

> . . . that is, the ways in which the popular classes assimilate what is offered at arm's length and recycle it in

> order to survive physically and culturally—from their
> uncertain relation to the state and their distance from
> technological development, to the persistence of elements
> that derive from oral culture and the maintenance of the
> popular apparatus for transmitting knowledge[38]

Martín-Barbero's view of popular culture provides Chicano film
theory with a more appropriate model of the dynamic between the
alternative and the mainstream. His explanations are particularly
relevant to the study of Chicano mainstream film production given the
fact that Chicano Cinema has an even closer relationship to the
Hollywood apparatus than the nationally backed cinemas of Latin
America. Chicano Cinema reaches an audience of Chicano and non-
Chicano North Americans who have been colonized by Hollywood and,
who as viewers, operate in a dialectical relationship to mass media. A
definition of the popular that does not reject mass culture but rather
explains how the apparatus of mass culture recasts ethnic culture for a
mass audience provides a clearer analysis of how ethnic culture relates
to the mainstream. Martín Barbero's view of mass culture approaches
the particular circumstances of Chicano feature filmmaking better than
the older explanation of *lo popular* advocated by filmmakers of earlier
decades.

The majority of Chicano feature film directors have, in most cases,
worked with Hollywood investors to gain distribution through
mainstream channels, and directors such as Luis Valdez, Cheech Marin
and Gregory Nava and Edward James Olmos have publicly identified
their films with the American mainstream. But utilizing the structural
conventions and means of production controlled by the mainstream has
not negated the possibility that their work can be received, consumed
or appropriated in a subversive manner. Chicano filmmakers have been
able to retain the progressive spirit of *lo popular* in their work. In some
cases they have been able to access huge audiences with very little
aesthetic compromise. Like the indigenous artisans of Latin America
who practice "cultural conversion" with increasing frequency, Chicano
Cinema offers an interesting example of a popular culture which
negotiates the formulas of mass culture with effective results.[39]

HOLLYWOOD AS A STRUCTURING SYSTEM
FOR ETHNIC CINEMA

The three legacies which Hollywood passes on to Chicano feature filmmaking are its long history of negative stereotyping, its use of genre as a structuring device and its power to generate popular myths. The first element, the prevalence of Hispanic stereotyping in Hollywood films, is a structuring system which Chicano filmmakers must confront at each phase of the filmmaking process; production, distribution and exhibition. The complex manner in which stereotypes permeate our perceptions has been articulated by Charles Ramírez Berg. He explains that Hollywood stereotypes no longer function as static representations but rather are "repeated, blended, countered and distorted"[40] by Hispanics and non-Hispanics alike.

Myth is another aspect of Hollywood cinema which Chicano directors deploy as a structuring system for their work. The intense appeal of Hollywood films engendered by their use of myth points to the power of the hero narrative to command an audience. But many stories of American heroes have historically served to justify North American expansionism and ethnocentric policies. These Hollywood myths reinforce U.S. government policies of control over Third World nations. The frontier myths perpetuated through the western genre films are examples of Hollywood legends which assuaged U.S. guilt for the massacre of thousands of Native and Mexican Americans. A concern of Chicano directors is to create a Chicano counter-myth which would reevaluate the ethnocentric belief systems of North America. By deploying alternative mythic heroes, a counter-myth is generated which creates a cultural anchor for Chicano self-expression and mobilization. The feature format offers a well tested vehicle to reach the masses.

Genre is the third construct of Hollywood filmmaking influencing Chicano feature directors and another aspect of Hollywood film which makes it so well liked by audiences. Edward Buscombe notes, "the conventions of . . . genre are known and recognized by the audience, and such recognition is in itself a pleasure. Popular art, in fact, has always depended on this."[41] From Buscombe's statement we can understand one of the central reasons why the Chicano Cinema Movement (a movement based in a "popular" approach to filmmaking) would opt to produce work within a generic system so firmly entrenched in dubious ideological work.

For nearly a century. Hollywood narrative formulas have organized audience expectations of what constitutes the boundaries of its genres. Most genres have distinct modes of narrative address which position the viewer in similar ways across films within the specific genre.[42] The argument can be made that the ethnic identity of the viewer is also a factor in the construction of generic modes of address. A genre film with "ethnic" characters can be understood as constructing the ethnicity of the viewing subject in order to transmit its ideological message. An example of this can be found in the Hollywood social problem films about Mexican Americans made in the Thirties, Forties and Fifties. The films were made from an Anglo point of view. They inscribed the white viewer into the text as a patronizing subject who offers the "option" of integration to the "troubled" Mexican American. In these films Mexican American subjectivity is constructed for the white audience and is necessarily shown to be passive and accepting of the integrationist proposition.[43]

If one looks at the appearance of the Mexican American image over the history of Hollywood genre films, it becomes evident that Mexican American characters have been limited to a few specific formulas, namely, the social problem film, the western and the gangster movie. Each of these genres is marked by its own set of stereotypes. Thus, by limiting the representation of Chicano identity to specific genres, Hollywood perpetually reproduces the stereotypes.

Nevertheless, though Hollywood thrives on reproducing itself, it does not depend solely on convention for its appeal. Difference is a fundamental principle of the cinema as a whole and genres rely on variation to achieve their effect. According to Stephen Neale, "The very existence of distinct genres illustrates this point."[44] The impulse towards difference is also driven by the economic aspects of Hollywood. Since film is an artistic commodity, each movie must boast its own uniqueness. Such need for innovative product may explain one reason why Hollywood embraces directors of color. The current upsurge in Chicano film production, could very well be evidence that Hollywood genres are exhausted and in need of variance.

The double layering of expectations, the regularized variety that leads to a definition of genre as process, has parallels to the structuring of Chicano identity vis-a-vis North American Culture. *Chicanismo* is more and more defined by Chicano artists as a hybrid identity which demands the transformation of North American influences into unique

Chicano forms of expression. Chicano filmmakers are exploring the possibilities of deploying Hollywood genres in the hopes of achieving a transformational cinema aesthetics. This transformation includes interjecting influences from the New Latin American Cinema Movement and other Third World Cinemas. By incorporating new visual and structural patterns coming from ethno-specific cultural practices like border aesthetics, *barrio* aesthetics and *rasquachismo* (techniques which will be explained in later chapters) into the mainstream of American culture, Chicano directors are projecting a distinct Chicano voice that is being heard on a national and international level.

NOTES

1. Contemporary Arts Museum, Houston, Texas, *Dále Gas/Give It Gas: The Continued Acceleration of Chicano Art* (Houston: Contemporary Arts Museum, 1977).

2. The mainstreaming of the Movement involved many factors including harassment by the Federal Bureau of Investigation, greater participation in electoral politics, increased access to middle class institutions by Chicanos and the growing influence of conservatism on the new generation of youth. The changing political outlook of the Chicano Movement is discussed at length in Carlos Muñoz Jr., *Youth Identity and Power: The Chicano Movement* (London: Verso, 1988).

3. Shifra Goldman and Tomás Ybarra-Frausto, *Arte Chicano: A Comprehensive Annotated Bibliography of Chicano Art, 1965-1981* (Berkeley: University of California Chicano Studies Library Publication Unit, 1985), p. 12.

4. Ibid., p. 19.

5. Rololfo Acuña, *Occupied America: A History of Chicanos*, 2nd ed. (New York: Harper and Row, 1981), p. 123.

6. The Brown Berets were the paramilitary arm of the Chicano Movement. They became the largest non-student radical youth organization in the Chicano community and played a significant role in bringing the street youth into the Chicano Movement. The orientation of the Brown Berets was that of a self-defense group. While they supported Chicano nationalism, they sometimes differed in their philosophy from other more Marxist nationalist groups. See Carlos Muñoz, *Youth, Identity, Power*, pp. 85-86.

7. Tomás Ybarra-Frausto, "Interview with Tomás Ybarra-Frausto: The Chicano Movement in a Multicultural/Multinational Society," in *On Edge: The Crisis of Contemporary Latin American Culture*, ed. George Yúdice, Jean Franco and Juan Flores (Minneapolis: University of Minnesota Press, 1992), pp. 207-216.

8. Carlos Muñoz Jr., *Youth, Identity, Power: The Chicano Movement*, (New York: Verso, 1989).

9. Antonio Ríos-Bustamante, "Latino Participation in the Hollywood Film Industry, 1911-1945," in *Chicanos and Film: Representation and Resistance*, ed. Chon Noriega (New York: Garland Publishing, 1992), pp. 18-28.

10. Media watchdog groups have been formed throughout Chicano history to protest and rectify unequal treatment. José Limón discusses this in his article, "Stereotyping and Chicano Resistance: An Historical Dimension," *Aztlán: An International Journal of Chicano Studies Research* 4, no. 2 (Fall 1973): 257-270. Two important Chicano groups dedicated to improving the image of Latinos in film and television were JUSTICIA, organized by Ray Andrade, Pete Rodriquez and Bob Morones at California State University - Los Angeles and NOSOTROS, founded by Ricardo Montalban in 1969. The Chicano Cinema Coalition also monitored Hollywood through its *Chicano Cinema Coalition Newsletter*.

11. Unlike what happened in the film and television industries, Chicanos had significantly more access to radio broadcasting. In 1946, KCOR became the first full time Spanish-language radio station to be owned by a Chicano. For a detailed account of Spanish language radio in the Southwest see Felix F. Gutiérrez and Jorge Reina Schement, *Spanish-Language Radio in the Southwestern United States* (Austin, Texas: The University of Texas Press, 1979).

12. According to a statement by Jesús Salvador Treviño, an Equal Employment Opportunity Commission report issued in 1969 found that only 3% of those employed by Hollywood studios were Chicanos. In public broadcasting stations nationally less than 1% were Mexican or Chicano. Jesús Salvador Treviño, "Chicano Cinema," *New Scholar* 8 (1982): 170-171.

13. For a listing of series titles and a brief description of their content, consult Treviño, "Chicano Cinema," and Harry Gamboa Jr., "Silver Screening the Barrio," *Equal Opportunity Forum* 6 (November 1978): 6-7.

14. Chon Noriega, "Road to Aztlán: Chicanos and Narrative Cinema," (Ph.D. dissertation, Stanford University, 1991), p. 73.

15. Ibid., p. 85.

16. Ibid.

17. "Pensamientos: Latinos and CPB: Quest of National Programming," *Chicano Cinema Newsletter* 1 (August 1979): 2-3.

18. Noriega, "Road to Aztlán," p. 90.

19. "DGA Figures on Days Worked by Women and Minorities," News Release, April 20, 1992, Directors Guild of America; *Variety*, April 21, 1992, pp. 1, 18.

20. *Chicano Cinema Newsletter* 1 (February 1979): 8.

21. Francisco X. Camplís, "Towards the Development of a Raza Cinema," in *Perspectives on Chicano Education*, ed. Tobias and Sandra Gonzales (Stanford: Stanford University Press, 1975), pp. 155-173.

22. Chon Noriega, "Between a Weapon and a Formula: Chicano Cinema and Its Contexts," in *Chicanos and Film: Representation and Resistance*, ed. Chon Noriega (New York: Garland Publishing, 1992).

23. Edward Said, *Orientalism* (New York: Vintage Books, 1979), p. 54.

24. Homi K. Bhabha, "The Other Question," *Screen* 24, No. 6 (Nov./Dec. 1983), p. 27.

25. Robert Stam, "Bakhtin, Polyphony and Ethnic/Racial Representation," in *Unspeakable Images: Ethnicity and the American Cinema* ed. Lester Friedman (Urbana: University of Illinois Press, 1990), p. 263.

26. Sarah Harasym, *The Post-Colonial Critic: Interviews, Strategies, Dialogues* (New York: Routledge, 1990), p. 66.

27. Stuart Hall, "Cultural identity and Cinematic Representation," *Framework* 31, (1989), p. 78.

28. Ibid., p. 70.

29. Personal testimony recorded by Néstor García Canclini and published in Néstor García Canclini, "Cultural Reconversion," in *On Edge: The Crisis in Contemporary Latin American Culture*, eds. George Yúdice, Jean Franco and Juan Flores (Minneapolis: University of Minnesota Press, 1992), p. 41.

30. Randall Miller, ed., *The Kaleidoscopic Lens: How Hollywood Views Ethnic Groups* (New York: Jerome S. Ozer, Publisher, 1980), p. 9.

31. Ibid., p. 10.

32. This was the case with Charles Burnette's film *To Sleep with Anger* which was marketed to a white suburban audience instead of to the urban black community which was the intended audience for the film. Lecture on "Blacks in the Media" by Charles Burnette, panel member at the Society for Cinema Studies Conference, Los Angeles, California, May 25, 1991.

33. Rosa Linda Fregoso, "Chicana Film Practices: Confronting the 'Many-Headed Demon of Oppression,'" in *Chicanos and Film*, ed. Chon Noriega (New York: Garland Publishing, 1991), p.170.

34. David Bordwell, Janet Staiger and Kristin Thompson, *The Classical Hollywood Cinema: Film Style and Mode of Production to 1960* (New York: Columbia University Press, 1985), pp.70-84.

35. Pamela Falkenberg, "Hollywood and the Art Cinema as a Bipolar Modeling System," *Wide Angle* 7 (Fall 1988), pp. 44-53.

36. Todd Gitlin, *The Whole World is Watching: Mass Media in the Making and Unmaking of the New Left*, (Berkeley: University of California Press, 1980), p. 3.

37. For further discussion of *lo popular* see Jesús Martín-Barbero, "Retos a la investigación de comunicación en América Latina," *Revista ININCO* 2 (Caracas), 1981.

38. Jesús Martín-Barbero, "Communication from Culture: the Crisis of the National and the Emergence of the Popular," *Media, Culture and Society* 10 (Fall 1988): 463.

39. Néstor García Canclini, "Cultural Reconversion" in *On Edge*, ed. Yúdice, Franco and Flores (Minneapolis: Minnesota University Press, 1992), pp. 29-44.

40. Charles Ramírez Berg, "Stereotyping in Films in General and of the Hispanic in Particular," *Howard Journal of Communications* 2 (Summer 1990): 12.

41. Edward Buscombe, "The Idea of Genre in the American Cinema," *Screen* 11, No. 2, p. 43.

42. Stephen Neale, *Genre (London: British Film Institute*, 1980), p. 25.

43. Chon Noriega, "Citizen Chicano: The Trials and Titillations of Ethnicity in the American Cinema, 1935-1962" *Social Research* 58, no. 2 (Summer 1991), pp. 412-438. It is important to note that Mexican American viewers could also have resisted being positioned by the genre by recognizing the conspicuous absence of a Mexican American point of view in the film.

44. Neale, *Genre*, p. 19.

II

DESTABILIZING ETHNIC STEREOTYPES: THE EARLY COMEDIES OF CHEECH MARIN

The formulation of the concept of stereotyping has been credited to journalist Walter Lippman.[1] He defined stereotypes as mental pictures created by people to interpret the world outside their reach. He stressed that the contents of an interpretation are factually wrong, products of faulty reasoning and that they tend to persist even in the face of knowledge and education. Since Lippman coined the term, extensive research into the prevalence and nature of stereotyping has been undertaken by sociologists.[2] After reviewing these studies, anthropologist Mahadev Apte states that four conclusions can be drawn concerning the nature of stereotypes. First, stereotypes seem to be present in all societies. Second, stereotypes can be positive or negative. Third, they can be directed towards others or self-oriented, and, fourth, stereotypes can involve a single trait or a configuration of many traits.[3] Charles Ramírez Berg points out that ethnocentric prejudice is what differentiates stereotyping from a common category-making process:

> The fact that the ingroup creates simplified symbols of the outgroup by selecting a few traits of the Other . . . pointedly accentuates differences. These negatively valued differences form the basis for making the Other inferior and excluding them from the ingroup.[4]

Along these same lines, Linda Williams suggests that the ethnocentric make up of stereotypes also serves the historical imperatives of the stereotyping group.[5] Thus, stereotypes are a key ingredient in the

27

hegemony of a society which maintains ethnocentric structures of power.

But the fact that stereotypes are used to maintain ethnic based controls in societies does not imply that stereotyping goes on without resistance. In the U.S., Chicanos and other ethnic groups deploy a variety of defensive proactive strategies to deflect and reshape negative stereotypes. By looking at how ethnic artists have manipulated negative stereotypes to their advantage, it becomes apparent that ethnic filmmakers can also position their work in a similar dialectical relationship to the phenomenon of stereotyping. In the case of the early Cheech and Chong comedies by Cheech Marin and Tommy Chong, one finds a highly skilled reworking of negative stereotypes. Through the use of humor, Marin creates a subversive subtext which undermines the power of caricatures and lays bare the falseness and the prejudicial nature of each stereotype.

ANTI-MEXICAN STEREOTYPES IN THE U.S.

The roots of anti-Mexican sentiment in North America can be traced back to the earliest days of its settlement. English colonization commenced at a time when hatred of Catholicism and Spain was at its worst. Mention of Spain conjured up the brutality of the Inquisition and atrocities of the conquistadors in the minds of Anglo settlers.[6] Radical Puritans who came from England were one of the most anti-Catholic and pro-nationalist groups to come to the New World. The Puritans ventured here with the goals of undermining Spanish commercial control and spreading the Gospel to American "savages." The hispanophobia propagated by the Puritans was a central element in their cultural teachings and served as a justification for their material domination of the indigenous population.

During the colonial period in U.S. history, English law was used to suppress the Spanish. Early exclusionary statutes banned priests and Jesuits. In New York, Catholics were forbidden to bear weapons and were required to pay a bond as security of good behavior.[7] Hostilities grew even more intense in the southeastern colonies where small wars were waged by the English against the Spanish, leading to Anglo control of the South.

By the first part of the nineteenth century, the United States had its eye on the Mexican territories in the Southwest. The established anti-Catholic and hispanophobic sentiments which fueled earlier expansionism also influenced the Anglo perception of Mexico. This hatred was combined with a distorted view of indigenous people whom Anglos regarded as "void of all goodness." Englishmen repeatedly accused the Mexicans of indolence, claiming that they did little to exploit their land: "If Christians had the inhabitation thereof, it would be put to a further benefit."[8] The negative stereotyping provided Anglos with a pseudo-moral argument for a second Mexican conquest.

Negative images of Mexico underwent a period of revitalization after the mid-18th century. North Americans read of indigenous rites of human sacrifice, devil worship and witchcraft.[9] Many Anglo-American histories relied heavily on the accounts of the Spanish conquerors Cortés and Gómara who were, of course, among the first Europeans to popularize disparaging depictions of the Mexican indigenous population to justify exploitation of them. The derogatory stereotypes were bolstered by "scientific" race theories circulating at the time. One of the more widely accepted theories which contrasted Northern peoples with those of Mexico and the southern hemisphere was called environmentalism. Environmentalists believed that all the great peoples and cultures of the world were found in the temperate zones of the planet. Accordingly, the closer a society lived to the equator, the less likely the possibility for human development.[10] Environmentalist writings characterized Mexican society as barbarous and savage.

Another racial theory used to justify stereotypes of the "inferior" Mexican was miscegenation. Miscegenation was a notion which held that the descendants of racially different parents inherited the worst qualities of each. The Mexican, being *mestizo* (of Spanish and Indian blood) was considered not only indolent, depraved and treacherous, but also unstable and prone to insanity or fits of rage because of his or her mixed blood heritage. A third theory common at the time was called manifest destiny. Its proponents used social darwinism to provide a convenient and seemingly invincible argument for imperialist wars. Darwin, himself, after having studied the westward invasions of Anglos into Mexico wrote:

> There is apparently much truth in the belief that the wonderful progress of the United States as well as the

character of the people are the results of natural selection.
The US was superior because its population was comprised
of the more energetic, restless and courageous men from
all parts of Europe.[11]

Although the propaganda of the period often represented its tainted
view of Mexican culture, actually, Anglo-Americans had little
significant contact with Mexicans until 1821 when Mexico gained her
independence from Spain and granted permission for US citizens to
enter the borderlands. Prior to 1821, fewer than 2500 persons of
European descent lived in Texas. This figure jumped drastically to over
20,000 during the next decade as adventurers, debtors and ambitious
Anglo farmers streamed in. As the number of Anglo-Texans grew, so
did their dissatisfaction with the Mexican government. Two key
events—the abolition of slavery in Mexico in 1829 and the prohibition
of further immigration from the US in 1830 led to open support for
secession from Mexico by the Anglos. Their actions culminated in the
Mexican American War. Proponents of the invasion argued that three
major advantages could be gained: potential mineral wealth, potential
black slave territory and potential brown peonage. Any guilty
consciences could be assuaged by the common belief that the Mexican
was an inferior race unable to take full advantage of his or her
country's magnificent resources. The U.S. won the war in 1848 and
embarked on a swift takeover of Mexican family lands by Anglo
ranchers and businessmen.

In essence, environmentalism and miscegenation and manifest
destiny provided European and U.S. aggressors with a biological
rationale for the Mexican American War. The various race theories
reinforced ethnic hatred as an ugly tradition in U.S. culture. This
tradition has yet to be broken. These racial theories have spawned a
series of negative Chicano stereotypes which have been deeply
imbedded in the national consciousness. Today stereotypes are
reinforced by the Hollywood film industry which uses negative Chicano
images for cheap laughs and cardboard villains. Anglo directed movies
have replaced the race theories of the past with equally damaging
propaganda by replaying negative stereotypes for millions of viewers
who otherwise have little or no significant contact with the Chicano
community.

OVERVIEW OF CHICANO STEREOTYPES IN FILM

Mexican men in early conquest/western novels were termed "greasers." They were characterized as lazy, dirty, stupid; victims of centuries of political chaos, priestly corruption and poverty. According to Arthur Pettit, "the final message of conquest fiction is that the only way the male Mexicans can survive is to accept a permanent inferior position to the conquerors."[12] The racist stereotypes which circulated in U.S. literature easily fed a host of ready-made characters into Hollywood which produced more that 300 "Mexican" themed movies during its first decade.[13] The most frequently used Mexican stereotypes in the early films were the bandido, the buffoon and the Latin lover. In the twenties, two more roles were added; the caballero and the gangster.

The Mexican Revolution served as a backdrop for many of the bandido films. An excerpt from a silent film shows the stereotyped dialogue spoken by one of the villains/buffoons in *The Bad Man* (1915):

> I keel ze man sis morning
> Hem call me dirty crook.
> I keel some more zis noontime
> And steal es pocketbook.[14]

Gary Keller suggests that the negative portrayal of rebels from the Mexican Revolution betrays a nervousness that Americans were feeling towards the socialist revolutionary activities across the border. U.S. corporations had heavy investments in Mexico, and the anti-imperialist rhetoric of the revolutionaries threatened to nationalize many of these U.S. held industries. In any case, by 1920, the revolutionary government of Mexico made its first public statement of disapproval of the distorted view of Mexico which had been promoted by Hollywood. The protest continued for many years, peaking during the Cárdenas administration which passed restrictions against importing offensive greaser movies. Mexican Americans also issued public statements of resistance against racist stereotyping. Many spanish language newspapers energetically protested derogatory depictions of Mexican Americans in early film and fiction.[15]

Nevertheless, the stereotyping went on unabated. Gary Keller notes that some of the most popular early silent films which stereotyped

Mexican Americans were the caballero films. The genre was established in 1914 with *The Caballeros Way* and carried on for several decades through the personages of Zorro, Don Arturo Bodega and the Cisco Kid. The heros in these stories were of pure Castilian blood. By stressing the European lineage of the protagonist the storylines in the caballero films created an ambiguity as to the Mexicanness of the characters. Indigenous Mexican features conveyed negative traits while European attributes signaled acceptance. Often the plots of these serials revolved around the hero vanquishing evil greasers who were in hot pursuit of an Anglo maiden. The Castilian hero saved her "virtue," but he seldom succeeded in marrying her. Thus, the story skirted the issue of miscegenation which the romance plot frequently implied.[16]

There also existed a subgenre of caballero films in the early 1930s which Gary Keller calls the gangster-greaser film. Leo Carillo played the stereotype of the gambling, murdering, extorting, pimping border bandido in more than twenty-five of these genre films. Compared to other gangster characters on the screen during that era, Carillo's character was more vile. Despite this stereotyping, Carillo was well respected by the Chicano Community and has a state park named after him in California.[17]

The bandido character was central to the depiction of Chicanos in the western film genre and a bloodthirsty symbol which still fuels the Anglo imagination of the region. In many western films the Rio Grande represents crossing over to a place where both the guilty and the wrongly accused can escape the Law (e.g. *Butch Cassidy and the Sundance Kid*). Most often the border crosser in westerns merely passes from one violent space to another. This is because it is not the side of the border that is important to the western, but rather, in the western genre the entire border region is delineated as a space where men who can't or won't fit into civilization go to act out their lowest desires. Clint Eastwood's "spaghetti" westerns and Sam Peckinpah's *Bring Me the Head of Alfredo García* and *The Wild Bunch* are strong examples of films which portray Mexico as a land which sanctions brutality.

Later westerns transformed the bandido into what Gary Keller terms a "brown avenger."[18] Following the lead of the blaxploitation films, characters like Mr. Majestyk were played by Charles Bronson as a half-Mexican and half-Slavic Vietnam vet who can single-handedly rid a town of gangsters and racists. Another example of a Mexican

American superstud character is Jorge Rivero in *Rio Lobo* who brings Arizona land grabbers to justice through retribution. In the nineties, one finds evidence of this bronze warrior stereotype in the film *Clear and Present Danger* in which a Mexican American military recruit is shown to have animal prowess as a mercenary fighter. While these warrior/avenger characters are portrayed as heros in the narratives, they still falter by their emphasis on violence as an integral aspect of the Chicano personality.

With the decline of the western, Chicanos were relegated to token parts in the background of Hollywood films until in the late seventies and early eighties when certain Chicano characters became the focus of gang movies. *Assault on Precinct 13* (1976), *Boulevard Nights* (1979), *Fort Apache the Bronx* (1980) and *Colors* (1985) are films which showed Chicanos as drug runners and murderous delinquents. Charles Ramírez Berg has pointed out that these Latino gang member/drug runner characters are the modern incarnation of the greaser/bandido types. Still driven by animalistic cravings, the gang member is particularly savage and brutal. Like the bandido, his nature dooms him to come to a tragic end. Reminiscent of the border region of the western, the urban settings for these gang films are mapped as sites where lawlessness and violence prevail.

On occasion Hollywood has deviated from the gangster/bandido stereotype, channeling perceptions of the Mexican as obsessive and passionate into the caricature of the Latin lover. Most often played in earlier films by Mexican actors Ramon Novarro, Ricardo Montalban, Gilbert Roland and Cesar Romero, the sexual appeal of these stars was attributed to their Latinness. Borrowing from the legacy of Valentino, Latin lover characters were suave, tender yet sexually dangerous. This stereotype can still be found today in Jimmy Smit's character in *The Old Gringo* which is typical of the latin lover. Smit is exceedingly exoticized in the role. His passion is so great that Jane Fonda (an old maid with no interest or sympathies for the Mexican Revolution) follows him across Mexico, risking her own death in the midst of battle. It is interesting to note that *The Old Gringo* was scripted by Mexican writer Carlos Fuentes and directed by Luis Puenzo who is from Argentina. The film provides an example of the way stereotypes are sometimes adapted by Latinos as a perceived positive characteristic of their own culture.

Other exceptions in the Hollywood pattern of negative male stereotyping occurred in a number of social problem films made during the 1930s and 1940s. In films of this genre, Chicanos are portrayed as sympathetic characters. However, while the scripts call for Chicano themed stories, the lead roles flounder from the lack of a Chicano point of view. Bringing an historical reading to the social problem genre and its use of stereotypes, Chon Noriega points out that many of the films of this genre were produced during the era of the Good Neighbor Policy. The effect of the political climate was to cause the Production Code Administration in its overseeing capacity to bifurcate issues pertaining to the Chicano experience in film into two components, Mexican and American. This meant that Hollywood would consider plot elements and character types against a yardstick of what impact they might have on a Mexican international market, not on the Chicano community.[19] Issues pertaining to racism were, thus, never interpreted from a Chicano perspective, leading to scripts which situated the Chicano characters as accepting of their lot in a larger Anglo world.

One case in point is the film *Bordertown* (1935). Actor Paul Muni plays Johnny Ramírez, a young Chicano who stoically forsakes success and all its corruption to return to the *barrio* where more practical ambitions can be realized. The end of the film insinuates that ambition is not part of Mexican identity. In *Right Cross*, Ricardo Montalban is a neurotic boxer whose unfounded bitterness towards Anglos is cured by the kindness of his manager's blond daughter (played by June Allyson). She convinces him that he can fit into white America, and, as a result of her speech, he then learns to adjust. More often than not, troubled Chicanos in the social problem films were unable to help themselves, and required intervention by a white good samaritan.

Unlike what occurred with male roles, the majority of female roles in Hollywood films were played by U.S. actresses of European descent. There were, however, several exceptions to this casting practice, most notably, the Hollywood careers of two Mexican actresses, Dolores del Rio and Lupe Velez.[20] Both actresses achieved a high degree of popularity with American audiences. Del Rio was one of Hollywood's top ten money makers of the 1920s.[21] But the financial success of these two actresses was largely based on the generic personas they portrayed. Del Rio was often cast as the "dark lady." While a stereotype, this image did not necessarily convey a negative type. Charles Ramírez Berg points out that because the dark lady character possesses sexual powers superior to her Anglo counterparts, she is positioned as more desirable in her films. But while the dark lady figure was shown to be superior to the Anglo, she, nevertheless, remained an oversimplification of the Chicana persona.

Another common Chicana stereotype is the half breed harlot. Ramírez Berg argues that in many films, the harlot is not actually of mixed blood but rather marked as different by her lower social status. Chihuahua (Linda Darnell) in *My Darling Clementine* is a classic example of this type. The harlot is usually played as a slave to her passions, unable to survive without a real man in her life. This stereotype differs greatly from a third Chicana type, the female buffoon.

The films of Mexican actress Lupe Velez supply typical example of the buffoon character. Her movies negate the Latin female's eroticism by making Velez an object of comic derision. Ramírez Berg explains how her role as female clown functioned in *Palooka* (1934):

> She is a big city vamp, a Latin golddigger who lures the rural prizefighting champ, Joe Palooka (Stu Erwin) into a life of fast-lane dissipation. Once again, her emotionalism and her inability to restrain her baser instincts—but instead to be controlled by them—conform with the common elements of Hollywood's stereotypical profile of Hispanic women.[22]

Commenting from a different perspective on the screen career of Velez, Ana López argues that Velez was:

> . . . outrageous, but her sexual excessiveness, although clearly identified as specifically ethnic, was subsumable. On and off screen, she, like Del Rio was mated with and married North American men.[23]

López mentions that the ethnic problematic displayed in Velez' early work—intermarriage, miscegenation and integration—could no longer be directly addressed in the films she made in the forties. The Good Neighbor Policy[24] (a U.S. government effort to improve relations with Latin America) dictated that Hollywood dump the more complicated, yet stereotyped sexual character played by Velez (and Del Rio) in favor of Portuguese/Brazilian actress, Carmen Miranda, whom López says functioned as a "surreal fetish" whose self-conscious artificiality drew attention to its own artificial otherness.[25] López gives much credit to Miranda for skillfully exacting numerous musical performances which draw attention to a ridiculous accent in such a way that she is able to call attention to the falseness of the Latin ethnicity coded into the stereotype she plays. In this way, Miranda undermined the buffoon stereotype which Velez had established earlier.

In discussing these female stereotypes it is important to mention the ambiguous nature of the ethnic characterizations. Often films with ethnic characterizations communicate a vague "latin" identity that erases distinct national identities. It is seldom possible to discern whether or not a character is Chicana or of other Latin American decent. This indifference on the part of Hollywood towards ethnic specificity can still be seen in films and television today. Take, for instance, the characters that appeared on the popular television program *Miami Vice* who were marked as non-specific Latino and Latina through stereotyping. The practice carries over to other ethnic groups as well in films which blur the culturally specific traits of various Asian and African peoples.[26]

I have omitted examples from films by non-Chicanos that portray Chicanos in a nonstereotypical fashion. There have been sporadic attempts at positive and genuine Chicano characters, such as in the films *Salt of the Earth* (1953), *High Noon* (1952), *Stand and Deliver* (1988), *Ballad of Gregorio Cortez* (1982) and *Milagro Beanfield War* (1988). Obviously these positive examples have not made inroads significant enough to battle the ignorance and opportunism of the producers of mainstream media. Unfortunately, the negative stereotypes of Chicanos remain, posing a formidable obstacle for Chicano filmmakers to reckon with.

As Chicano and Chicana filmmakers embark on the difficult task of constructing their own cinematic identity they necessarily inherit the baggage of Hollywood stereotypes. Some directors confront the Hollywood legacy by creating positive Chicano hero figures. Other Chicano directors have opted to construct complex characters using techniques of psychological realism. Cheech Marin has taken the unusual route of using the very same Chicano stereotypes entrenched in Hollywood and turning them on their head through subversive comic techniques. His strategy of deploying negative images to undermine false codes of ethnicity which have structured Anglo perceptions over centuries poses an innovative solution to the problem of ethnic self-representation in the Hollywood mainstream.

STEREOTYPES AND ETHNIC HUMOR

Ethnic humor is usually understood as a mechanism through which a member of a certain cultural group refers to persons of a different cultural group in a disparaging light by playing upon traits or behavior stereotypically associated with the targeted group.[27] Studies have shown that outwardly directed ethnic jokes are made in all cultures and typically refer to the other as stupid, ignorant or unclean.[28] When ethnic humor is used by a more powerful group in society to make fun of a minority sector the function of that humor is usually to rationalize various discriminatory practices by the privileged group. For example, derogatory jokes told by Anglos about Blacks and Mexicans in the U.S. often serve to justify racism.[29]

The general psychological framework that has been applied to derogatory ethnic humor is the concept of ethnocentrism. A useful explanation of the term is provided by Madadev Apte:

> . . . attitudes of ingroup adulation and outgroup hate, stereotyping and prejudice must all be considered to be concomitants of ethnocentrism. Treating or thinking of other cultures and people as inferior, for example, is one way of strengthening self-image. Prejudice reinforces ethnocentrism, just as negation of the cultural values of other people nurtures self-esteem and feelings of superiority.[30]

Apte also mentions that intergroup conflict and control is exacted when ethnics are ridiculed if they do not conform to existing cultural norms. Ethnic humor, he says, exerts its oppressive powers by stressing that ethnicity is permanent and cannot voluntarily be discarded. Because of this, ethnocentric humor has been presumed to be an expression of a human need to vent hostility and aggression. But several social psychologists have taken issue with this position challenging the notion that one can automatically assign malicious intent to the joke teller. Edward Oring asserts that individuals and groups who narrate ethnic jokes do not necessarily accept the negative or pejorative stereotypes of the target group.[31] From a similar perspective, R. Middleton expresses his view: "even if a person does not accept the validity of a stereotype, he may be willing to suspend his disbelief temporarily in order to enjoy the humor of the joke."[32] This supposition, that ethnic humor directed from outside towards a minority does not always imply racial hatred on the part of the speaker, may have some validity. But, in the final instance, it ignores the central ethical question of how the derogatory ethnic joke harms the targeted ethnic community or individual.

A further context for ethnic humor is when it is used by the ethnic community from its position as the outgroup as a cultural weapon against the majority culture. Freud's theory of how the hostile joke functions as a challenge to authority provides a useful form of reference to understand this type of ingroup ethnic joking. According to Freud, stereotyping (what he refers to as caricature) in hostile jokes is often funny because the stereotypes represent a "rebellion against authority, a liberation from its pressure . . . we laugh at them . . . because we count rebellion as a merit."[33] For Freud, caricature is the act of taking one or a limited number of traits and exaggerating them. Often the degree of incongruity between the reality and the stereotype is very high. In Chicano culture the following joke provides an effective example of humor being used to undermine the dominant Anglo culture and its presumption of superiority over Chicano culture:

> An Anglo is left in charge of a Chicano crew assigned to go down into a cesspool and pass buckets of sewage up to him. Instead, when the boss returns, he finds the Anglo in the cesspool passing the buckets up to the Chicanos. Asked to explain, the Anglo replies, "I ain't takin' no shit from no Meskins!"[34]

Several classic examples of ethnic humor used by an oppressed minority to wound their tormentors can be found in African American culture. Lawrence Levine has put together an excellent study of Black laughter as an oppositional tool. He shows how Blacks have manipulated stereotypes of "the man" in order to confront his hatred.[35] Levine recounts how South Carolina Blacks in the 1940's were still telling the story of a supposed exchange between the racist politician Ben Tillman and a Black delegate during the state Constitutional Convention of 1890:

> Tillman had delivered a speech in which he disparaged
> South Carolina's Black population. The Negro delegate
> arose and denounced Tillman, who the next day responded
> in an even stronger speech during which he roared "Why
> you dirty black rascal, I'll swallow you alive." "If you do,"
> his black antagonist shouted back, "You'll have more
> brains in your belly than you've got in your head."[36]

Levine also narrates an a joke told inside the African American
community which skillfully reverses stereotypes about a Black maid and
her white employer who have both given birth to their babies on the
same day:

> One day the white woman runs into the kitchen crying out
> in delight, "Oh, my baby said his first word today!" The
> Black baby in the basket on the kitchen floor looks up and
> asks, "He did, what'd he say?"[37]

While ethnic humor is most often associated with jokes that poke
fun at ethnicities outside the humorist's own group, ethnic humor can
also be directed inwardly as well. This occurs most frequently for the
purpose of cultural maintenance by poking fun at members of the group
who seek to assimilate into the majority culture. In the Chicano
community such humor takes the form of *agringado* joking.[38] These
jokes ridicule Chicanos who have become too "gringoized" (or too
North American) in their attitudes and actions. Self-derogatory ethnic
jokes seem to flourish in cultures that have been marginalized.
Especially well researched are the uses of self- critical ethnic jokes in
Jewish and African American communities. A significant number of
these studies of self-directed humor have tended to interpret such
behavior in a negative light. Relying on a reductionist theoretical
approach by which all ethnic humor is seen as socially aggressive,
researchers concluded that self-derogatory humor was masochistic, a
sign of self-hatred and revulsion. Edward Oring has challenged this
view by noting that such approaches failed to distinguish a simple
communicative act from artistic expression. He added, ethnic jokes are
primarily structures of ideas to be perceived intellectually. They are
based on the creation and perception of an appropriate incongruity.[39]

Along these same lines, cultural theorist Sandy Cohen argues that ethnic stereotypes can be cultivated by the ingroup as a means of group identification and moral support:

> Such jokes reflect the social conditions of the minority: they show conflicts within the group, reinforce acceptable behavior and ridicule deviance from the group norm. The large amount of hostile jokes seems to indicate an American need for ethnic origins and stereotypes, serving not mere revenge for humiliation but also the examination of one's own value system by comparing it to the values of the majority.[40]

Cohen points to the frequent use of irony in ethnic jokes by ethnic sectors who choose to replicate negative stereotypes of themselves in their jokes. Trickster stories brought to the U.S. in the Old World folklore of immigrants exemplify this. Thus, we have the Jewish schlemazel waiter who because he is "inept," "accidentally" spills hot soup on the patronizing customer. In Black culture, the joke is told of the slave who, because he is "incompetent," burns down his master's new barn. By employing the stereotypes used against him or her, the ethnic minority can confront the fact that the majority will never see him or her as they truly are. Cohen adds that Jewish jokes allow the group "not to say we as a group are like that, but rather, we as a group are perceived as being like that and we know it."[41]

In using self-directed stereotypes the ingroup can also comment on the pressures it feels to assimilate into the majority culture. Américo Paredes has done a fascinating study of jokes told by Chicanos about Mexican folk medicine.[42] The jokes center around the character of the *curandero* or folk healer. The *curandero* is the butt of most of these jokes. His medicinal treatments are often portrayed as absurd and lewd. (Many of the folk cures call for the use of violent purgatives.) But at the same time the *curandero* figure is ridiculed for his outdated reliance on indigenous beliefs (to the point where sometimes the treatment is more harmful to the patient than the illness), the joke also exposes the gringo health care system as just as bad, if not worse. In the *curandero* jests, the patient is often forced to seek the free help of the folk healer after being turned away by a U.S. hospital or threatened with a needless operation by a greedy Yankee doctor. Paredes remarks on the double nature of these jokes:

In satirizing of folk medicine and *curandero* belief tales, they express a mocking rejection of Mexican folk culture; in their expression of resentment towards American culture, they show a strong sense of identification with Mexican folk traditions.[43]

COMIC USES OF THE *PACHUCO* STEREOTYPE

Chicano artists have always used humorous stereotypes in a critical and self-reflexive way. One of the first groups to do this was the Teatro Campesino. Founded in 1965 by Luis Valdez, the son of Mexican migrant workers, Teatro Campesino became the cultural extension of the United Farm Worker's Movement.[44] Many of Valdez's actors were non-professionals. They worked through improvisation to create short agit-prop skits he called *actos*. Each *acto* relied heavily on comedy and satire for its effect,[45] and contained a political message exposing a specific problem of the farmworkers.

Valdez described his style of humor and his dependence on comic types in the early *actos* as somewhere between Brecht and Cantinflas. Brecht, he felt, motivated him to deal with history and politics through distancing devices that forced the audience to think. But in a careful analysis of the construction of characters in the *actos*, Juan Castañon García points out that Brechtian characters were much different than those of the Teatro Campesino.[46] According to Castañon García, Brecht hoped to disguise his characters, whereas the characters in Teatro Campesino were group archetypes. In Valdez's plays the characters even hung signs around their necks to make sure the audience could identify them. What worked as an alienating technique for Brecht, served as a method of group identification and unity for the strikers. Castañon García sees the origin of the *actos* more rooted in the slapstick and burlesque style of the Mexican comic Cantinflas who played a trickster type character in dozens of low budget Mexican films of the forties and fifties. Much of Cantinflas' humor evolved from his inability to speak the standard Castilian Spanish of the elite. In attempting to do so, he would accidentally cast insult on anyone of higher social standing. Cantinflas was also a very physical comic whose techniques greatly influenced the comic style of many Mexican films which are readily available for viewing in the United States.[47]

Los Vendidos (The Sellouts) was one of the earlier *actos* to be performed by Teatro Campesino. It was eventually filmed for television in 1973. It is set on a simple bare stage dressed with only a single sign in the corner reading "Honest Sancho's used Mexican Lot and Mexican Curio Shop." As the *acto* opens we see Honest Sancho dusting off his human mannequins, each with a sign around his neck. There is the revolutionary, dressed in a Pancho Villa era costume, the *pachuco* wearing typical street clothing and the farmer (*campesino*) in modest working clothes. The first shopper to enter the store is Miss Jimenez. She pronounces her name Jim-enes, emphasizing the Anglo accented pronunciation. The audience recognizes her as an assimilationist. She has come to buy a Mexican because she works for Governor Reagan's office and they need a token brown face for a luncheon. Honest Sancho offers her the *campesino*, "the volkswagen of Mexicans" but she wants something more sophisticated so he shows her Johnny Pachuco. Johnny is a *vato loco* (crazy dude). Sancho tells us Johnny does everything he needs to do to survive in the city—including stealing and using a knife. He can resist arrest and makes a wonderful scapegoat. When brought to life, Johnny struts downstage and lets out a "Fuck You" to the audience. Further traits of this *pachuco* are his inferiority complex and his love of marijuana. When Johnny shows Miss Jimenez how good he is at stealing by snatching her purse, she remarks, "We can't have any more thieves in the State Administration."[48]

The play ends with a twist. Miss Jimenez finally pays $15,000 for a character who plays the revolutionary. He suddenly goes crazy yelling slogans in Spanish and turning on the other mannequins who chase Jimenez out of the store. Sancho then, himself, turns into a puppet. We discover that Sancho has been the real mannequin all along used by the others to "rip off the man" by selling phony Mexicans. The *pachuco*, revolutionary and *campesino* divide up the money and go out to a party. The audience sees that stereotypes were self-imposed in order to make gains over the dominant culture.

Los Vendidos is an example of one of the earliest uses of the *pachuco* character in Chicano theatre. The representation of the street smart youth continued to fascinate Valdez and Teatro Campesino for many years, culminating in the theme of their hit musical *Zoot Suit*. *Pachuquismo* was invented by the urban Mexican American youth of the forties as a means of self-expression. They developed their own slang called *caló* and took on the zoot suit fashion popularized by Black and Filipino Americans. According to Valdez, the *pachuco* was rough and often dangerous, but was still admired by most Mexican American youth because he was a rebel who made a statement against racial injustice by calling attention to himself.

SELF-DEROGATORY STEREOTYPING IN THE CHEECH AND CHONG FILMS

Richard "Cheech" Marin, a third generation Mexican American from Los Angeles, is perhaps the most experienced Chicano feature film director to have ever worked in Hollywood.[49] He and his former partner, Thomas Chong, who is of Canadian and Asian heritage, starred in and directed over a half dozen popular comedies in which Marin plays a streetwise Chicano doper.[50] In 1987, Marin went solo to write, direct and star in *Born in East LA*, a film in which he changed his character to an average working class Chicano played with a more naturalistic acting style.

Marin's rendition of the *pachuco* in the Cheech and Chong films is quite different from the character in Valdez's plays. Cheech's streetwise doper might be more accurately described as a *cholo*. It is a contemporary term which, like *pachuco*, was adopted by Chicano youth from the *barrios*. *Cholos*, like their antecedents, the *pachucos* or zoot suiters, are associated with *la vida loca* (the crazy life) and call each other *vatos locos*. According to Luis Plascencia, life in the fast lane for the *vatos* can range from innocuous acts of adolescent rebellion to more serious activities involving drugs, alcohol or crime. Cheech's character is often dressed in the garb of the *cholo*—khaki pants, a long sleeved plaid shirt buttoned to the neck over a sleeveless muscle shirt, and a bandanna or stocking cap pulled down to the eyebrows. Cheech's body language imitates the cool swagger of the *vatos* and his dialogue echoes their *caló*.

Luis Plascencia provides an interesting social history of how the categories of *pachuco* and *cholos* became popularized among Chicanos in the seventies.[51] Plascencia stresses that the true identity of the *pachuco* was formed during the forties as a response to many factors affecting the Mexican community including growing urbanization, the development of juvenile delinquency and the existence of Chicano youth

clubs formed to block attempts at forced assimilation. Plascencia says
that the historical specificity of this identity has been lost over the
decades as Chicano artists, playwrights and poets have romanticized the
pachuco into a potentially revolutionary figure. He points out that one
of the major promoters of the *pachuco* as a transhistorical icon was
Low Rider magazine which ran articles that distorted the actual role of
the *pachucos* in history.[52] By writing most of its articles in *caló* and
by using the terms *pachuco* and lowriding interchangeably, *Low Rider*
popularized the *pachuco* image on a mass scale for youth in the
seventies causing many readers to refer to themselves as *pachucos*.

The term *cholo*, according to Plascencia, had been used in the
Southwest since the early 1800's to refer the Mexican of *mestizo*
heritage. It was an offensive term denoting an individual as
quarrelsome and vicious. Later it was used to refer to Mexicans who
had recently immigrated to the US and had assimilated very little. In
the seventies, certain low riders who belonged to formal car clubs used
the term *cholos* in a derogatory manner to refer to deviant low riders
who "gave good respectable low riders a bad name."[53] The *cholos*, in
turn, had a negative view of the formal car club members. *Low Rider*,
says Plascencia, chose to limit references to the term *cholo*, preferring
to project a homogenous image of the Chicano as *pachuco*. In effect,
it absorbed the *cholo* identity into a broader cultural symbols of the
pachuco and *pachuca*.

Ironically, it appears that from Plascencia's study that the
glorification of the *pachuco* in the seventies in low rider culture lead to
the elevation of the mythical *vato loco*, "*el pachuco*" above the
contemporary vato loco, *el cholo*. The zoot suit was embraced as the
emblem of Chicano expression in many of Low Rider's stories while
cholo dress received lesser attention. Plascencia criticizes *Low Rider's*
appropriation of positive cultural symbols because he says their
intentions and uses of these symbols were contrary to the needs of *El
Movimiento* (the Chicano Movement). *Low Rider's* ownership
transformed the pachuco image into a commodity for the purpose of
selling more magazines and more advertisements. They published ads
from ultra conservative beer companies which displayed models posing
in zoot suits. The point of Plascencia's article is to show that
pachuquismo and the *cholo* style were genuine symbols of Chicano
working class culture that, nevertheless, were appropriated by
corporations and divested of their socio-historical context.

When Cheech Marin plugs into the low rider character in *cholo* dress it appears at first glance that he is stereotyping *pachuquismo* (the culture of the *pachucos*). But there are ambiguities in Cheech's character that differ from the mythical image of the *pachuco* adopted by the low riders and Luis Valdez. Unlike the heroic *pachuco*, Cheech's character does not hang out with other Chicanos or low riders in the *barrio*. He is that piece of the Movement that got into drugs not politics. And while he does not consciously resist Anglo culture, he still manages to foreground his Chicano identity. In the end, the humor in these films arises from his street smarts and his "otherness" in such a way that he effectively dismantles the stereotype he so cleverly portrays.

Marin's Cheech and Chong films have always been aimed at a general audience and have been very successful at the box office. *Up in Smoke* was the highest-grossing comedy of 1978. Marin claims that his films are popular because of his style of comedy that makes a positive moral statement by bringing up important social issues beneath the mask of humor:

> I've always said that my method is to slip the message into your coffee. You don't taste it. It goes down smooth, but later you feel the effect.[54]

The Chicano that Marin plays is a doper who has some street smarts. The opening sequence in *Up in Smoke* sets up the character type he will portray in all his early comedies. He awakens on his living room couch surrounded by a hoard of kids watching cartoons. Still drowsy, he stumbles to a filthy bathroom. Toilet paper is hanging out of the toilet. Dirty clothes litter the floor. He finally opens his eyes to find that he has been urinating in the hamper. He then saunters out the front door of his dilapidated house. In the yard are several other Chicanos cutting their hair. Cheech crosses the street and admires his "ride." The opening music, "Low Rider" (by the group WAR) comes up as the film cuts between detail shots of the car, its fringe, its stenciled windows, its chain fashioned steering wheel and its crushed velvet interior. Cheech slides down in the front seat, starts the engine and eases his low rider down the street out of frame.

Cheech cruises down the California freeway. He sings "My baby's so fine, I do it to her nearly all of the time." He then comes upon two blond "chicks" sunbathing by the side of the road. Seeing them, he responds by immediately crossing into oncoming traffic, but the blonds refuse his offer of a good time. Undaunted, he soon spies two giant breasts down the road. Cheech exclaims, "Hey honey bend over, I'll drive you home," and heads across traffic again. The breasts, it turns out, belong to Tommy Chong (Cheech Marin's side kick). In the film, Chong plays an Anglo doper who is just as crude, dirty, unemployed and oversexed as Cheech's character. Even more degenerate than Cheech, Chong spends all of his time selling or smoking dope. Chong is the stereotype of the Anglo hippie. His character is rebelling against his parents who are wealthy suburbanites. In one scene, while sipping their afternoon cocktails, Chong's parents demand that Chong get a job. The father says he knows someone at United Fruit (one of the major exploiters of Central American labor, implicated in the CIA takeover in Guatemala and also one of the principal partners of RCA when it was founded) and threatens to put Chong to work in the fields as a banana picker. Chong, dressed in his dirty jeans, headband and wireframes, gives his dad the finger and heads for the beach.

Other ethnic characters in the Cheech and Chong films are similarly stereotyped. In *Up In Smoke* there is the character of Curtis, Cheech's African American neighbor. Curtis is a jive-talking con man, outrageously dressed like a Hollywood version of a black pimp. His character constantly tries to hustle Cheech. In one of Curtis' scenes he sells waiter's uniforms to Cheech's Chicano band members as their band costumes. Other stereotyped characters include the narcotics detective with Stacey Keach cast in the role. He is costumed with a burr haircut and a tightly cropped moustache which draws attention to his thin upper lip. Keach wears polyester pants that fit him too tightly, complementing his patronizing and abusive personality. Like Curtis, the Detective is a one-dimensional character. He has only a single desire—to make the big bust. Another ethnic stereotype in the mix is a Japanese American character named Toyota Kowasaki. In *Still Smokin'* there is a stereotyped nordic woman. She is beautiful but also intimidating because of her imposing size. Bigger than both Cheech and Chong, she plays a chamber maid with a sex drive that leaves the two men begging for mercy.

When every ethnic group is exposed to such equal ridicule, the negative effect of the stereotype in the film is altered. In the case of Cheech and Chong movies, the ethnocentric aggression that stereotypes typically imply is diffused. All ethnic groups are shown to be equally vulnerable to being typed, equally susceptible to becoming the butt of an ethnic joke. This technique encourages the viewer who recognizes himself or herself as one of the caricatured ethnics in the film to read the Chicano stereotype in the same way he or she would most likely read a stereotype of his or her own ethnic group in the film—as an ethnic caricature with little basis in fact. This type of cinematic dismantling forces viewers to draw comparisons and promotes recognition of the existence of stereotypes across ethnic groups.

Another technique in the Cheech and Chong films which disarms the stereotype for the viewer is the attitude of playfulness maintained in their films. Their style of comedy is very cartoonish, and most of their humor relies on exaggerating to the point of absurdity. For instance, *Cheech and Chong's Next Movie* opens with the two dopers stealing a garbage can full of gasoline. They decide to pour it in their gas tank without a funnel. Gas and garbage spill all over the two of them. They act like no one can see them, but this is all going on at a busy intersection. Nonplussed, they start to drive away. Cheech jokes with Chong, "Oh shit man, I'm going to be late for work again, man. That's the fifth time I've been late this week and it's only Tuesday, man." Then Chong lights up a joint, and the interior of the car explodes. In the next shot, the two are covered with cinders, clothes are shredded and eyebrows are seared. The clownish "Wiley Coyote and the Road Runner" tone serves as a barometer for the rest of the film. The attitude conveyed by scenes such as this is silliness. The broadly drawn world which inhabits each of the films firmly establishes a make believe space for the viewer. The relationship of the viewer to the comic situation is, therefore, a qualified one, which works along the lines of Freud's description of audience positioning in joking situations. Freud posits that a feeling of superiority on the part of the joke listener does not arise if he or she knows that the joker has only been pretending to ridicule himself or herself.[55] Cheech and Chong leave little room for naturalism in their acting style, their mise-en-scene and their plot structures. They are constantly returning to the absurd so that any audience member would be hard pressed to deny fantasy aspects of the film.

Cheech's character in these movies is generally unfavorably stereotyped. Nevertheless, he does display a few redeeming qualities. First, he is usually smarter than Chong. Many jokes will be played out by having Chong say something totally ridiculous. The joke is then followed by a reaction shot of Cheech whose face mirrors the audience's own "I can't believe this guy" response. This happens in *Cheech and Chong's Next Movie* when we find out that Chong thinks his dope dealing is going well because he says he sold a couple of joints yesterday; "to himself." Cheech's double-take response matches our own. Because of these double-takes the audience tends to identify more with Cheech, the Chicano, and his superiority over Chong, the non-specific Anglo.

A second redeeming feature of Cheech's *vato* stereotype is his disrespect for authority. For decades, this trait had been tied to the bandido, greaser or gangster Chicano stereotypes in mainstream Hollywood films. But the trait had been scripted into these movies as negative examples of incorrigible lawlessness. In Marin's films, he turns disrespect for the law into healthy rebellion, converting his Chicano character into a sort of trickster. In *Cheech and Chong's Next Movie* one finds a typical example of this. Cheech manages to steal his boss's van by pretending not to understand English spoken by the security guard. Another example of undermining authority appears in *Up In Smoke*. Cheech is in the men's room with the narcotics detective who does not recognize Cheech as the drug dealer he has been pursuing. Cheech maintains his cover by playing the clown, making silly references to his own penis. When Cheech leaves, we find out that during the bathroom performance, Cheech has been urinating on the detective's leg.

In a later scene, Cheech subverts the law as he is going through Customs. While waiting at the border check point, he makes a lewd comment to several nuns in the next car and receives their frigid stares in return. As the border agent approaches Cheech's car, Cheech panics because he's smoking a joint. He tosses it out the window without seeing that it lands on the lap of one of the nuns. The sisters are quickly apprehended by the border agent in place of Cheech. There is then a shot of the nuns smiling in excitement as they are being frisked. Ironically, Cheech's lascivious desires come to fruition at the hands of the border authorities.

In a previous section of this chapter, it was mentioned how the stereotype of the Mexican American emphasized his vulgarity and "uncivilized" nature. In an attempt to disarm the stereotype, Cheech and Chong make vulgarity one of the central comic tactics of their movies. Using many references to bodily functions in their films. *Up*

In Smoke contains a scene in which Cheech gets the runs after eating Mexican food. He frantically searches for a toilet. While holding his buttocks he mutters, "Come on cheeks, stay together." In *Cheech and Chong's Next Movie* there is a scene where Chong tricks Cheech into drinking from a jar of urine. When Cheech realizes what he is drinking, he goes crazy and spills the urine all over himself screaming, "Oh god, I'm gonna die" as his van swerves down the street.

Freud's theory of jokes provides a useful explanation of humor which relies on bodily degradation for comic effect. Such jokes, he says, work because the listeners recognize that all humanity is equally subject to the same bodily functions. He interprets grotesque humor in the same manner that he explained the obscene joke. Such jokes work by unmasking inhibitions imposed upon the listener. In the case of Cheech and Chong films, the precarious nature of white protestant civility is exposed and, in turn, the accusation by the "civilized" group that the "other" is barbaric and grotesque is disclosed as a contradiction. In this way the dirty Mexican stereotype is turned on its head. The vulgar stereotype is further confounded as Chong's baser side is also foregrounded. In *Cheech and Chong's Next Movie*, Chong urinates through the bathroom window on to the bald head of their Anglo neighbor. *Still Smokin'* includes a scene at the end of the film where Cheech and Chong are performing on stage. The scene is set around one dog's (Cheech) excitement at seeing the other dog (Chong) defecate.

Hollywood has traditionally shown Chicano sexuality in terms of the Latin lover stereotype or bandido/rapist so that Chicano eroticism is portrayed as either perverted or exotic. Marin plays with the stereotype of the oversexed latin. He constantly offers himself to women by making crude statements such as his comment to Chong in *Up In Smoke*, "I hope she hasn't eaten. I got something for her. Tube steak smothered in underwear." In an ironic twist, instead of being offended, most of the women characters in Marin's films take him up on his offers. To his surprise, the Cheech character finds out that these women are usually sexually freer and more insatiable than he. In *Nice Dreams*, Donna, an old girlfriend, invites both Cheech and Chong up to her apartment to have sex with her. In *Still Smokin'* the Dutch chamber maid uses both men for sex and then sends them crawling away from her bedroom exhausted. Any hint at a threat to these women characters is dispelled because the women are just as sexually aggressive as Cheech is. They are untainted by false conceptions of Chicano sexual stereotypes and, therefore, force us to see the stereotype as a hollow image.

Another way that Marin's films manipulate stereotypes is by alluding directly to the Anglo media's portrayal of Chicanos. For example, in *Up In Smoke*, Cheech wanders on to the set of a Hollywood film called *Wamba's Revenge*, a typical Chicano gang film. This scene can be read as an indirect allusion to the film *Walk Proud*, a bronze exploitation film which drew public protest by Chicanos when it was released. On the set of the film there is a Chicano character dressed in a zoot suit who holds a knife to the neck of a terrified white girl. A racist director and his crew encourage the actors to exaggerate their lines. The scene finally ends when Cheech sends a lost actor to crash through the wall of the set. Thus, Cheech sabotages the racist movie production.

Cheech makes another direct critique of Hollywood in *Cheech and Chong's Next Movie* when he composes a ballad about Chicanos. Chong accompanies him on guitar with a Mexican folk melody as Cheech sings the first two verses:

> Mexican Americans
> Don't just like to get into gang fights
> They like flowers and music
> And white girls named Debbie too.
>
> Mexican Americans
> Are named Chata
> And Chela and Chema
> And have a son-in-law named Jeff.

And the last verse:

> Mexican Americans
> Don't like to go to movies
> Where the dude has to wear contacts
>   to make his blue eyes brown,
> And don't it make your brown eyes blue.

When Cheech is through singing, he tells Chong, "It's like a protest tune." The song highlights Hollywood's misrepresentation of Chicanos and foregrounds diversity in identity. The song also crystallizes a dominant theme in the Cheech and Chong films. In these films, the Chicano is someone who knows he is stereotyped and always tries to resist by showing he is aware of the typing. At the same time, being Chicano means interacting with Anglo culture without giving up Chicano aspects of identity. This Chicano identity, though stereotyped in many negative ways, still confronts assimilation as Cheech consciously marks himself with his *cholo* dress, his *caló* and his low rider style. Thus, Marin's approach to ethnic humor parallels the self-aware style of humor that is found in Jewish and African American culture. He presents an effective analysis of derogatory stereotypes which destabilize ethnic categories and the ethnocentric power structures they maintain.

Other regressive elements of American culture are alluded to and questioned in Marin's comedies. In *Cheech and Chong's Nice Dreams* Cheech gets rich from selling dope out of a low riding ice cream truck. He has a mansion on a beach front populated by topless blond sunbathers. His character arrogantly jokes about becoming a sun king (allusion to the Aztec god central to the Movement's ideology) who throws joints to the natives. He dresses in the casual attire of a successful California capitalist. But immediately Cheech pokes fun at his character's cool pose, undercutting the glamour attached to achieving upper-class status. In the midst of American opulence, Cheech falls back on his underdog "Chicano" ways. From his mansion, he orders four bottles of "Fussy Pussy" wine as he cooks tortillas to make "Mexican pizza." Later he meets his old girlfriend, Donna, who invites Cheech and Chong back to her apartment for sex. As Cheech and Chong are on her bed, Donna's biker husband, "who is known to hate Mexicans," comes home and chases the nude Cheech throughout the building. Then, as Chong helps Cheech escape, it is discovered that Cheech has stupidly accepted a check from an Anglo in exchange for all the cash they've made dealing. In the final scene, Cheech and Chong are forced to take jobs as male exotic dancers. They call their act "The Sun Kings in Paradise." Thus, Cheech's desire to fit into the capitalist mold, to naively trust the Anglos with his aspirations, results in his downfall and humiliation. The humorous effect of this comic situation is somewhat similar to the way Paredes says the *curandero* jests work:

> It releases a complicated set of conflicting emotions
> ranging from exasperation to affection in respect to
> the unacculturated Mexican American.[56]

By drawing attention to his character's inability to "blend in" to the Anglo way of life, Marin makes ethnicity more than just throw away humor. Utilizing the Sun King references, Marin cleverly shows how the symbols of the Movement can easily be coopted and how the hegemony of capitalist society structures Chicano behavior by creating an horizon of accepted desires and aspirations.

Marin's critique of American social norms also encompasses the Chicano Movement. In *Cheech and Chong's Next Movie*, Cheech is waiting for his Chicana girlfriend to show up for a date when he falls asleep and has two dreams. In the first dream, Cheech is dressed in a zoot suit from the forties. He suavely enters an elegant boudoir where Donna is glamorously shown lounging on a bed. Cheech takes Donna in his arms but is awakened moments before they can make love. He soon has his second dream in which he is dressed as an Aztec priest. He approaches his girlfriend who appears as a dead Aztec maiden awaiting sacrifice on an Aztec temple monument. Cheech fondles her breasts and intends to rape her, but is soon awakened once again. In mocking the image of Aztec manhood which had become a frequently used icon in Chicano murals, Marin takes a bold step and calls into question the sexism embedded within neo-Aztec mythology. Marin's use of satire works in this scene as a double-edged sword. In this film and in the other Cheech and Chong comedies, self-derogatory ethnic stereotypes serve as an internal monitor for the community as well as an indictment of falsehoods imposed from the outside. If it is an instrument for attacking the enemy, satire is also an instrument for keeping the tribe in line.[57]

CONCLUSION

Anti-Mexican stereotypes are deeply rooted in the consciousness of white America and have served to justify the economic and cultural domination of Aztlán. In U.S. film, the image of the inferior Mexican became entrenched in Hollywood movies as greaser, bandido, buffoon, peon, gangster, dark lady and rapist. Chicano community groups and the State of Mexico published statements of protest and outrage against these slanderous and demeaning stereotypes. Later, with the emergence of the Chicano Art Movement, the negative stereotypes came under further scrutiny. The image of the *pachuco* which had been previously abused was embraced by Teatro Campesino and transformed into a heroic symbol of Chicano identity.

In mainstream film, the Chicano street youth stereotype surfaced in the movies of Cheech Marin. Cheech's character was not really a *pachuco* in the same sense that *pachuquismo* had been used by *Low Rider*, Teatro Campesino and the Chicano Art Movement. But by extending the lineage of *pachuquismo* to the low riding *cholos*, one can see Cheech's character fits within the *pachuco* identity framework. Yet, the subtle differences in Cheech's stereotyped character differentiates it from other representations of the type in Chicano culture. His *vato* is not heroic, and has little politicized consciousness. Nevertheless, his self-derogatory portrayal—though embodying many of the same negative traits which have been attributed to Mexicans by colonizers over the past five hundred years—does not project a masochistic or demeaning image of the Chicano. This is because the nature of the humor in his films contextualizes stereotypes. All ethnic groups, including Anglos, are typed in equally absurd ways. Marin's broadly drawn comic technique, similar to that used by Teatro Campesino, forces the audience to consider that ethnic stereotypes are ridiculous and not based in truth. His trickster-type antics appeal to the viewer as he challenges authority figures and institutions like the Hollywood movie industry that profit from such false images. In Cheech and Chong films, self-derogatory humor also provides a mirror for the Chicano community to look critically at itself by comparing traditional values with new problems.

Groups that have been targets of racial stereotyping have always been faced with the need to generate positive counterimages with their art. Sometimes this results in a kind of "image policing" by ethnic artists and critics who are quick to condemn any type of negative character depictions by ethnic artists.[58] But Plascencia's study of *Low Rider* magazine's promotion of the *pachuco* myth has shown that, even though an ethnic image is positively constructed, there is no guarantee it will be used for the good of that community. What Cheech Marin's early comedy films show is that an ethnic director can take a negative stereotype and, through humor, expose the stereotype as racist and unfounded, thereby, initiating the process of undermining its significance for a general film audience.

NOTES

1. Mahadez Apte, *Humor and Laughter: An Anthropological Approach* (Ithaca: Cornell University Press, 1985), p. 113.

2. For an extensive bibliography of research on stereotyping see J.C. Brigham, "Ethnic Stereotypes," *Psychological Bulletin* 76 (Fall 1982): 15-38.

3. Apte, *Humor and Laughter*, p. 114.

4. Charles Ramírez Berg, "Images and Counterimages of the Hispanic in Hollywood," *Tonanzín* 6, (Nov. 1988): 12.

5. Linda Williams, "Type and Stereotype: Chicana Images in Film," in *Chicano Cinema: Research, Reviews and Resources*, ed. Gary Keller (Binghamton: Bilingual Review/Press, 1985), pp. 94-108.

6. Charles Gibson, ed, *The Black Legend: Anti-Spanish Attitudes in the Old and New World* (Durham, N.C.: Duke University Press, 1971).

7. Paredes, "Origins of Anti-Mexican Sentiment," p. 143.

8. Ibid., p. 149.

9. *The Traveller* (Woodbridge, N.J.: James Parder, 1758).

10. William Robertson, *The History of America* (New York: J. Harper, 1977 reprint of original 1832 addition).

11. Ibid., p. 312.

12. Arthur Pettit, *Images of the Mexican American in Fiction and Film* (College Station, Texas: Texas A & M University Press, 1980).

13. Gary Keller, "The Image of the Mexican in Mexican, United States and Chicano Cinema: An Overview," in *Chicano Cinema*, p. 20. For further discussion see Allen Woll, *Images of the Mexican American in Fiction and Film* (Los Angeles: University of California Press, 1977); Linda Williams, "Type and Stereotype: Chicana Images in Film," in *Chicano Cinema*, pp. 94-107; Blaine P. Lamb, "The Convenient Villain: The Early Cinema Views of the Mexican-American," *Journal of the West* 14 (October, 1975): 75-81; and Carlos Cortés, "Who is María? What is Juan? Dilemmas of Analyzing the Chicano Image in U.S. Feature Films," in *Chicanos and Film*, pp. 83-105.

14. George Roeder Jr., "Mexicans in the Movies: the Image of Mexicans in American Films, 1894-1947," unpublished manuscript, University of Wisconsin, 1971, p. 27.

15. See José E. Limón, "Stereotyping and Chicano Resistance," pp. 257-270.

16. Imperialist culture evinces a persistent obsession with the theme of the dark man raping the white woman. See Angela Davis, *Women, Race and Class* (New York: Random House, 1984).

17. The Chicano community has characteristically reacted sympathetically to the plight of Chicano actors who are cast in stereotypical roles. For instance, in 1979, after the release of *Boulevard Nights*, the Chicano Cinema Coalition published an article denouncing the racist stereotypes depicted in the film, while at the same time praising the "fine acting" of the Chicano and Latino actors in the film. "CCC Releases Statement on *Boulevard Nights*, Louis R. Torres, ed., *Chicano Cinema Newsletter* 1, no. 3 (May 1979): pp. 3-4.

18. Keller, "The Image of the Chicano," p. 27.

19. Chon Noriega, "The Trials and Titillations of Ethnicity in the American Cinema, 1935-1962," *Social Research* 58 (Summer 1991): 413-438.

20. Ana López, "Are All Latins from Manhattan: Hollywood, Ethnograhpy and Cultural Colonialism," in *Unspeakable Images*, ed. Lester Freidman (Urbana: University of Illinois Press, 1991), pp. 404-424. For a reference guide of actresses who portrayed women of color in Hollywood film see Maryann Oshana, *Women of Color: A Filmography of Minority and Third World Women of Color* (New York: Garland, 1985).

21. George Hadley-García, *Hispanic Hollywood: The Latins in Motion Pictures* (New York: Citadel Press, 1990), p.39.

22. Charles Ramírez Berg, "Stereotyping in Films in General and of the Hispanic in Particular," *Howard Journal of Communications* 2 (Summer 1990), p. 12.

23. López, "Latins from Manhattan," p. 419.

24. At the urging of the State Department Office of Inter-American Affairs, Hollywood executives agreed to make movies which promoted good relations with Latin America. During the period from approximately 1939 to 1947 more than eighty films dealing with Latin America were produced.

25. Ibid., p. 419.

26. See also "Who is María? What is Juan? Dilemmas of Analyzing the Chicano Image in U.S. Feature Films," in *Chicanos and Film*, ed. Chon Noriega (New York: Garland Publishing, 1992), pp. 74-94.

27. See Mahadev Apte, *Humor and Laughter*, p. 108.

28. Ibid., p. 46.

29. See George Myrdal, *An American Dream* (New York: Harper, 1944).

30. Apte, *Humor and Laughter*, p. 42.

31. Edward Oring, "Everything is a Shade of Elephant: An Alternative to a Psychoanalysis of Humor," *New York Folklore* 1 (Fall 1973): 149-159.

32. Russell Middleton, "Negro and White Reactions to Racial Humor," *Sociometry* 23 (Fall 1973): 76. An example where this theory might apply is in the Cheech and Chong video *Get Out of My Room* in which Chong is asked how he met Cheech. He responds, "Well, he was my gardener, see..." In the

context of the film, the audience clearly understands that Chong bears no hostility towards his long time friend.

33. Sigmund Freud, *Jokes and Their Relation to the Unconscious* trans. James Strachey, (New York: Penguin, 1960), p. 148.

34. José Reyna, "Contemporary Myths in Chicano Joke Tradition," in *Renato Rosaldo Lecture Series 3: 1985-1986*, ed. Ignacio García (Tuscon: Arizona Board of Regents, 1987), p. 27.

35. Lawrence W. Levine, *Black Culture and Black Consciousness* (New York: Oxford University Press, 1977).

36. J. Mason Brewer, *Humorous Folktales of the South Carolina Negro* (Orangeburg, S.C., 1945) p. 7.

37. Levine, *Black Culture*, p. 67.

38. See Limón, "Stereotyping and Chicano Resistance: An Historical Dimension," pp. 257-270.

39. Oring, "Everything is a Shade of Elephant," p. 159.

40. Sandy Cohen, "Racial and Ethnic Humor in the United States," *Amerika Studien/American Studies* 30 (Fall 1985), p. 203.

41. Ibid., p. 204.

42. Américo Paredes, "Folk Medicine and Intercultural Jest," in *Introduction to Chicano Studies*, eds. L.I. Duran and H.R. Bernard (New York: MacMillan, 1973), pp. 104-119.

43. Ibid., p. 271.

44. The United Farm Worker's Union was started by César Chávez in 1965 to protect the rights of Mexican American and Filipino American migrant farm laborers. The leadership was very effective in organizing a national consumer boycott of grapes and lettuce which drew international attention to their organization. For a detailed history of the Farm Workers Movement see Ronald B. Taylor, *Chavez and the Farm Workers* (Boston: Beacon Press, 1975).

45. For a close analysis of satire in the work of Valdez and other Chicano writers see Guillermo Hernandez, *Chicano Satire: A Study in Literary Culture* (Austin: University of Texas Press, 1991).

46. Juan Castañon García, "Bertolt Brecht and Luis Valdez: The Relation Between the Self and the Techniques in their Theatre," *De Colores: Journal of Chicano Expression and Thought* 5, (1980): 98.

47. Another famous Mexican comic was Tin Tan whose style was quite similar to Cantinflas. Tin Tan actually started in Mexican films playing the character of a *pachuco*.

48. Jorge A. Huerta, *Chicano Theatre: Themes and Forms*, (Ypsilanti: Bilingual Press, 1982), p. 64.

49. In an interview, Marin revealed that he had co-directed the films he made with Tommy Chong. Marin never received credit as director for those films. But when one considers that Cheech and Chong worked by

improvisation, the conclusion that Marin exerted a significant directorial influence over his films is reasonable. Dennis West and Gary Crowdus, "Cheech Cleans Up His Act," *Cineaste* 16 (July 1988), p. 37.

50. *Up in Smoke* (1978), *Cheech and Chong's Next Movie* (1980), *Cheech and Chong's Nice Dreams* (1981), *Cheech and Chong Still Smokin'* (1983). They also starred in and wrote *Things are Tough All Over* (1982) and *The Corsican Brothers* (1984).

51. Luis F.B. Plascencia, "Lowriding in the Southwest," in *History Culture and Society: Chicano Studies in the '80's*, eds. National Association for Chicano Studies (Ypsilanti: Bilingual Press, 1983), pp. 137-159.

52. Plascencia gives evidence that such was not really the case. Ibid., p. 148.

53. Ibid., p. 153.

54. West and Crowdus, "Cheech Cleans Up His Act," p. 37.

55. Freud, *Jokes*, p. 260.

56. Paredes, "Folk Medicine," p. 272.

57. William W. Cook, "Change the Joke and Slip the Yoke," *Journal of Ethnic Studies* 6 (Spring 1978): 113.

58. See Salim Muwakkil, "Spike Lee and the Image Police," *Cineaste* 17 (April 1990): 35, for an explanation of how this problem relates to African American filmmaking.

III

MYTHIC PROPORTIONS: CREATING *RAZA* HEROES IN *ZOOT SUIT* AND *LA BAMBA*

MYTH IN THE EARLY WORKS OF LUIS VALDEZ

In 1967, after working for two years with the United Farm Workers, Luis Valdez and the Teatro Campesino decided it was necessary to separate from the union in order to establish themselves as a truly authentic *teatro del pueblo* (people's theater). This distance from the demands of the picket line allowed Valdez to develop a new poetic consciousness, an approach to theater fundamentally different from the agit prop immediacy of the earlier slapstick plays he had done for the union. With a broader, more diverse audience, Teatro Campesino evolved into a new kind of theater, one comprised of *mitos* or myth plays which emphasized "secular spirituality." In Valdez' words:

> Not a *teatro* composed of *actos* or agit prop, but a *teatro*
> of ritual, of music, of beauty and spiritual sensitivity. A
> *teatro* of legends and myths. A *teatro* of religious
> strength.[1]

The focus of Valdez' *mitos* was on developing a Chicano psychic memory and subconscious myth structure. Taking Chicano art in this new creative direction was applauded by elements of the Movement who desired a more universal orientation for *Chicanismo*, but others saw this transformation to a mythic theater dedicated to a neo-Mayan philosophy of mystic love as a betrayal of the political goals and proletarian origins of *La Raza*.[2] Thus, Valdez's theories became the focus of a debate on Chicano cultural determination.

THE IMPORTANCE OF MITOS
TO THE CHICANO MOVEMENT

Early on, the cultural arm of the Chicano Movement resurrected an Aztec legend of origins known as Aztlán and transformed it into one of the most vital elements of the nationalist struggle. The legend and its use among peoples of the Southwest has a long history. There is speculation that ancient Aztec elites who had migrated from what is now the U.S. southward into central Mexico used the story to justify their brutal treatment of the native peoples already inhabiting the area. The Aztecs told the story that their god Huitzilopochtlí had instructed them to leave Aztlán, their ancestral home in the southwest United States. They were to search for the promised land to the south and would come to recognize it by the appearance of an eagle resting on a nopal plant devouring a serpent. On that site they built their empire, what is now called Mexico City. Several generations later, their former homeland to the north which they called Aztlán grew in mythological stature and came to be known to the new culture as their paradise lost.

The rebirth of the Aztlán myth in contemporary Chicano thought is credited to Chicano poet Alurista who spoke about it to students at San Diego State University in 1968.[3] Its popularity spread quickly and, within a year, Aztlán was used as the central inspiration for the manifestos of the Chicano Movement, most notably "El Plan Espiritual de Aztlán." Underscoring Aztec origins, the Chicano student activists who authored the plan used the myth to build a nationalist movement among students:

> We the Chicano inhabitants and civilizers of the northern land of Aztlán, from whence came our forefathers . . . we are the nation, we are a union of free pueblos, we are Aztlán."[4]

Aztlán was a powerful tool for mobilizing the Movement. According to Michael Pina its political significance was twofold:

> The mythic narrative of Chicano nationalism weaves two distinct strands of human understanding into a single fabric.

> It fuses the pre-Hispanic myth of Aztlán to the modern
> myth of history: on one level Chicano nationalism calls for
> the re-creation of an Aztec spiritual homeland, Aztlán; on
> another, it expresses the desire to politically reconquer the
> northern territories wrested from Mexico in an imperialist
> war inspired by Manifest Destiny.[5]

The Chicano Movement's relation to the myth was and still is
particularly powerful because Aztlán became a regenerative symbol.
Aztlán became a "living myth" and self-evident truth for the
nationalists.[6] Eventually, the myth of Aztlán organized daily
consciousness for many Chicanos. It began to provide identity, location
and meaning, and an intellectual space where unity was possible. The
concept of Aztlán furnished both a geographic homeland as well as a
spiritual one with its emphasis on the indigenous roots of the Chicano
nation. Images from Indian cultures like the black UFW eagle drawn
in the shape of an inverted pre-Columbian pyramid, and the images of
the indigenous aztec warriors functioned as icons of empowerment. In
this way, Aztlán serves as a touchstone of truth, an ultimate reference
point.

Along with Aztlán, the term La Raza was adopted by many
Chicanos signaling a new pride in a native heritage that had previously
been denied by many. The concept of La Raza came from the writings
of Mexican intellectual José Vasconcelos who developed the theory of
la raza cósmica (the cosmic or super race) arguing that the mixture of
Spanish and Indian races created a superior race of people in Latin
America.[7] The Chicano orientation towards the La Raza, however,
stressed the indigenous rather than the Spanish influences on Mexican
American culture. When you consider that relatively few Spaniards
came to the New World, and that they came to conquer the indigenous
people, the identification with Indian culture is particularly appropriate
and important.

Searching for his own cosmic union with his Indian ancestry, Luis
Valdez and Teatro Campesino mounted several *mitos*. In these pieces,
there was frequently a blending of indigenous gods (i.e. Huitzilopochtlí,
Tonantzín, Quetzalcoatl) with Christian deities (i.e. Jesus Christ and the
Virgin of Guadalupe). Valdez felt that this attempt at syncretism would
better communicate the principle of the golden rule (espoused by
Mayan philosophy) which served as the core of his own neoindigenous
belief system. According to Jorge Huerta, the *mitos* helped Chicano

audiences to get in touch with their indigenous roots by drawing connections between native myths and familiar Catholic allegories.[8]

After several years of successfully producing the *mitos*, Valdez decided he wanted to reach a more general audience and set about mainstreaming his work. Nevertheless, the influence of the *mito* story and structure remained strong in his productions. In 1976, Valdez created a new play, *Zoot Suit*, which would end up on Broadway. *Zoot Suit* was a Chicano musical allegory that used mythic elements to tell the story of the Servicemen's Riot in the 1940's (known as the "zoot suit riots" to Anglos). In 1981, Valdez prepared a screen version with the same title, and shot it on a limited budget of three million dollars in front of a live audience at the Aquarius Theater. Six years later, Valdez released his second feature film, *La Bamba*, a musical biography of Chicano teenage rock legend, Ritchie Valens, which also deployed myth but in much more subtle ways.

The decision of Valdez to move into feature films as a vehicle for constructing myth was a logical cultural strategy. Of all the modern art forms, cinema and television are the most intimately connected to myth. Because of its persistent use of archetypal characters, Hollywood narrative approaches myth more closely than it does historical realism.[9] Feature films easily rework history into myth, impelling the public to incorporate Hollywood rewrites of American culture into their belief systems. The phenomena of the Rambo revision of Vietnam during the 1980s exemplifies this.[10]

Many of the myths that are disseminated by Hollywood films often exist in the culture prior to the creation of a film. It is the previous exposure to the myth which increases the power of the film to grip the audience. This is the case with movies by Valdez and his use of Chicano myth. Valdez incorporates myths such as *pachuquismo* and Aztlán; belief that have already been embraced by much of the Chicano community. But as he uses his film to popularize Chicano myths for a general North American Audience, the degree of penetration will undoubtedly vary according to what extent the audience is tied into the Chicano belief system or are susceptible to the spirit of the myth.

ZOOT SUIT AND THE *PACHUCO* HERO

The film *Zoot Suit* is based on the story of a Mexican American youth who was one of a group of *pachucos* (street youth) wrongly convicted of murder in what became a sensationalized case in the early forties known as the Sleepy Lagoon Trial. Valdez uses the trauma of the incident to hurl his protagonist, Henry Reyna, (played by Valdez's brother Daniel in the film) into a quest for his own identity and a higher level of consciousness. During his search, Henry is forced to confront his alter-ego personified in the film through the character of El Pachuco, powerfully played by James Edward Olmos.

The movie is shot as if we are watching a play. El Pachuco struts on stage before a packed house and cautions, "Our *pachuco* realities will only make sense if you grasp their stylization," adding, "It was the secret fantasy of every *vato* to put on the zoot suit and play the myth." In this eloquent opening monologue, Valdez sets up El Pachuco as the intellectual and spiritual guide of the film. El Pachuco is also our visual guide in *Zoot Suit*. In many instances, he controls the editing by commanding Henry to move to a new scene. Often a cut is initiated with a snap of El Pachuco's fingers. In a way, he is a metaphor for the Chicano director who has, at last, gained control of the lens and now influences our perceptions of the cinematic reality.

We meet Henry Reyna in the next scene. It's 1941. Henry was set to report to the Navy the following day, but, instead, is about to be arrested for the murder of a Chicano youth. The scene is lit with a single spot. El Pachuco comes out of the shadows poised sardonically behind Henry's shoulder. He taunts Henry for ever thinking that the Navy would value a Chicano soldier. "*Muy* (very) popeye the sailor man, *ese*." He warns Henry, "Your war's on the home front," but Henry refuses to listen. The scene then quickly shifts. Henry is being beaten by racist cops. El Pachuco stops the action with a snap of his finger. He tells Henry to be strong enough to take it. El Pachuco brags that he has taught Henry to survive. "Escape through the *barrio* streets of your mind," he says. Then, as all is silent on stage, El Pachuco leads Henry back home to his family to the night before this incident took place.

At his home, we see Henry and his younger brother putting on their "drapes" (the zoot suit). El Pachuco, visible only to Henry, stands in a cool pose in the background. When Henry leaves the room, El

Pachuco hands him a switchblade. The world of El Pachuco is inherently violent. When Henry accepts the knife he begins his initiation into the *pachuco* code. The following scene is set in the kitchen. The boys' father arrives home from work while their mother makes beans and tortillas. The father tells his sons not to dress in the zoot suits. "It invites trouble," he adds. He also scolds them for calling themselves Chicanos, "It means you're trash." The father in this scene is representative of a more traditional generation. He offers words of advice that the sons cannot accept because of the particular set of circumstances that confront them as Chicano youth. The scene underscores the fact that Chicano youth consciously adopted their look and way of life as a consequence of their need for self-expression and comments on the generational shift in identity politics during the Forties.

In the next scene, Henry and four of his friends are in jail. A white liberal lawyer comes to defend them. The five give the lawyer a hard time, challenging his motives with their indifference, until he warns that they'll all be sent to the gas chamber. This harsh reality breaks through Henry's tough facade. But as Henry's about to accept the lawyer's help, El Pachuco stops the action. He tells Henry that a trial won't make a difference. Henry argues that they need a lawyer and asks El Pachuco, "Whose side are you on anyway?" "The side of the heroes and the fools," El Pachuco replies. El Pachuco refuses to play any part of the farce they call "American justice." The ultimate nationalist, El Pachuco is conveyed as an extremist in his cynicism, yet, at the same time, heroic in his tragic defiance of racial injustice. The audience knows El Pachuco is right in theory, but he is also a dangerous fool who is willing to risk Henry's life to get him to follow him. Like the Devil figure in medieval morality plays (and in earlier *mito* plays by Valdez) El Pachuco uses clever arguments to steal Henry's soul.

The film shifts next to a dance that took place the night of the murder. Valdez stages a musical number which is interrupted by a fight between Henry and a rival Chicano. At the climax of the clash, El Pachuco appears and stops the action again with a snap of his fingers. He advises Henry, "not to hate your *raza* (people) more than you love the gringo. That's exactly what the show needs, two more Mexicans killing each other." Henry then looks out at the audience, exposed and embarrassed as Valdez gives us a shot of the audience looking back at

Henry. We learn from this scene that El Pachuco is remarkably calculated and precise in his political analysis of the situation. The scene implies that violence is political. The scene also serves to incorporate the audience (the Chicano community) as a character in the film. Their appearance in the narrative forces the main character, Henry, as well as the viewer to reflect on the story from a Chicano communal perspective.

The next scene is set in jail. Alice Bloomfield (played by Tyne Daley) introduces herself as the chairperson of Henry's defense committee. Henry is cold towards her and tries to intimidate her with his *machismo*. Insulted, she leaves. Henry is quickly confronted by El Pachuco who mocks Alice more bitterly than Henry did. El Pachuco then teases Henry for being attracted to the "white broad." El Pachuco's macho attitude towards her is offensive which makes Henry's character appear gentler. The macho stereotype played by El Pachuco is effectively juxtaposed with the real *pachuco*, Henry, in that brief moment. But in the next instance, Henry is antagonized by El Pachuco's threats to his manhood and tries to one up El Pachuco by putting on a harsh *pachuco* attitude. Immediately, El Pachuco restores his authority over Henry and the drama. Exerting an eerie bravado, El Pachuco warns Henry, "Don't try to out *pachuco* me, *ese*." At this point, Henry appears to be totally at the mercy of his *pachuco* alter ego who, suddenly, whips out a switchblade and hurls it into the next set, thereby redirecting the action and inserting Henry back into the narrative. Thus, El Pachuco proves he is bigger than life; *pachuco* to the core, more brutal, more honest, more original and stylish then anyone else on the stage or in the audience.

Valdez cuts to this next scene on the sound of the switchblade lodging in the desk of a courtroom prosecutor. He then shows us a shot of the audience which is now composed of Henry's family as well as those who were shown earlier as patrons of the play. In this way, Valdez establishes a double reality: the cast and audience in the film are audience as well as jury. The scene also foregrounds Henry's own double consciousness. In a courtroom Henry comes to realize that he is not only a Chicano but is positioned as a stereotype of a Chicano by the judge and jury. An expert witness is called to the stand and testifies that Mexicans have an inborn characteristic to use knives passed down to them from their Aztec forebears. In response, El Pachuco whispers to Henry, "Put on your feathers, *ese*. They're going to fuck you."

Valdez then cuts to a new scene giving us a shot of El Pachuco playing a "Marijuana Boogie" at a piano with three *pachucas* singing alongside him. Henry appears in the scene too. El Pachuco quips, "This is 1942 or is it 1492?" and then, "There're no more pyramids, only the gas chamber." This is a biting commentary on racism and the inevitability of tragedy befalling Henry. It sheds light on Valdez' myth/reality juxtaposition by associating the *pachuco* story with ancient history of the Aztec downfall, thereby further politicizing the *pachuco* myth.

Testimony is later given by Henry's girlfriend Dela. Valdez transports us to the sleepy lagoon setting where we find out that Henry did not commit the murder. Instead, Valdez shows us a shot of Henry watching El Pachuco beat an invisible victim incessantly with a wooden beam. The act is shot in slow motion so that the gesture comes to represent the paradoxical violence of El Pachuco's character. The violent action against another Chicano at the lagoon contradicts El Pachuco's earlier attempts at stopping Henry from fighting at the dance. In this scene El Pachuco does not act for the good of his *raza*. Valdez's mythic warrior is shown as a flawed hero, not a simple icon of cultural separatism.

At the close of the trial, Henry is sentenced to life. While imprisoned, he falls in love with Alice Bloomfield. Though she cares for Henry, she cannot reciprocate. He suffers a deep humiliation from her rejection. El Pachuco appears and chides Henry for going out on a limb with her. "You turned yourself into a victim." As if triggered by what El Pachuco says, Henry reacts with violence, lashing out against a prison guard, getting himself thrown into solitary confinement. The scene cuts to the complete and terrifying darkness of Henry's holding cell. The blackness is only broken when El Pachuco strikes a match and offers Henry a joint. Eventually, Henry, desperate and broken, pulls himself together by thinking of his family. In the scene, Valdez gives us a shot of Henry as he sees his family seated in the audience. But just as Henry seems to be reclaiming his dignity, El Pachuco soon reminds Henry of his prison reality. Henry's familial vision dissolves. El Pachuco is once again a self-destructive force, challenging the healing value of *la familia* (the family) with his self-centered skepticism.

The scene ends with a climactic moment of realization as Henry confronts El Pachuco. "I know who you are," he says. "You're the one who got me here. You're my worst enemy and my best friend." At this moment, Henry comes to terms with his double consciousness. The films tells us that it may have been his *pachuquismo* which allowed him to survive racism. Yet as a protective identity, *pachuquismo* is also self-destructive and oppressive. Henry recognizes that El Pachuco is his own world view, his *pachuco* pride which has lead him to set himself apart from the Anglo world in search of a unique identity, a mythic consciousness. The moment of awareness is brief as the scene is once again interrupted by El Pachuco who takes control of Henry and the filmic narrative. "Don't take the play so seriously," El Pachuco smirks, a cue for everyone in the audience to laugh at Henry who has let down his guard in a brief moment of self-reflection.

After this scene, El Pachuco, who previously had only been seen by Henry, becomes visible to the Anglo characters in the play. Compelled to redeem himself, El Pachuco challenges a group of sailors on leave. They engage in a bloodthirsty chase of El Pachuco. The scene echoes the brutality of the Servicemen's Riots in 1943 when hundreds of GIs raided the *barrios* to beat and strip *pachuco* youth.[11] In a moment of ritualized self-sacrifice, El Pachuco throws away his knife and heads for the stage.[12] There, the sailors attack him. When they move back from his body, we see a naked man crouched in shame. We think he is El Pachuco but the scene cuts quickly so that the body of El Pachuco becomes that of Henry's younger brother. Henry reaches into the frame to console him. As he leans back out of frame, the camera reveals that the crumpled man is once again El Pachuco who rises defiantly wearing only a loin cloth and crucifix around his neck. The brother/El Pachuco has been transformed into a mythological figure, the dignified and heroic Aztec warrior facing a contemporary European invasion. The scene inserts *pachuquismo* into an historical continuum of Chicano repression and resistance.

The movie ends with Henry's release from prison. The reunion with his loved ones is momentarily interrupted by the appearance of El Pachuco in a dazzling white zoot suit on a platform atop the stage. In this culminating scene, El Pachuco's costuming marks him unmistakably as the ancient god Tezcatlipoca, the Aztec deity of wisdom. His physical placement on the stage above the action, prompting Henry to look up in awe, his omniscient yet fallible interplay with Henry's fate, his magical ability to appear anywhere at anytime, and his symbolic stance confronting the Servicemen combine to elevate El Pachuco's character to mythic stature.

Henry looks up in admiration and recognition. The film cuts to various cast members giving their version of what happened to Henry after his release. The police say Henry became a drug addict and returned to prison. Alice says he married Dela and had five children who call themselves Chicanos. His brother says Henry became a war hero. These various stories serve as reflections from the ideological mirrors directing our perception of Chicano identity.

El PACHUCO AND THE MYTHIC
CONSTRUCTION OF IDENTITY

The idea of transforming El Pachuco into a symbol of Chicano identity by reclaiming him as myth was regarded as a problematic strategy by some Chicano artists and scholars. Rafael Grajeda points out that most Chicano poets who have written about the *pachuco* resist the temptation to romanticize him. They portray the *pachuco* as a nihilist, the victim of drug addiction and violence.[13] Octavio Romano's research also exposes contradictions in using a *pachuco* myth as a foundation for building a more overreaching Chicano myth. He interprets the actual phenomenon of *pachuquismo* in the 1940s as essentially existentialist:

> The Pachuco Movement was one of the few truly separatist movements in American History. Even then, it was singularly unique among separatist movements in that it did not seek or even attempt a return to roots and origins. The Pachuco indulged in self-separation from history, created his own reality as he went along even to the extent of creating his own language . . . For the Pachuco . . . separated himself from history, and in doing so became transformed into Existential Man.[14]

Romano's thesis prompts the question, if the *pachuco* was separating himself from history, did Valdez misrepresent *pachuquismo* by linking it to a myth of indigenous origins? If that is the case, what are the cultural advantages and political pitfalls of establishing connections between *pachuquismo* and the Aztlán myth that may never have been there for the original *pachucos*?

Frantz Fanon warned against creating myths which are more imagined than real. He cautioned that these romanticized myths constitute false utopian narratives of the past and often encourage retreat into exoticism and passivity.[15] Fanon advised that instead of leading the people astray with over-idealized cultural visions, the cultural producer should serve as an "awakener" of his/her people.

> Stories, epics, and songs of the people are now beginning to change . . . There is a tendency to bring conflicts up to date and to modernize the kinds of struggle which the stories evoke . . . The method of illusion is more and more widely used. The formula, this all happened long ago, is substituted with that of what we are going to speak of happened somewhere else, but it might well have happened here today, and it might happen tomorrow.[16]

I conclude that Valdez, though perhaps guilty of creating his own *pachuco* reality has skillfully used *pachuquismo* in a manner similar to that advocated by Fanon. One should take into account that, although Valdez turned the *pachuco* into a hero, he did not dangerously romanticize him. The *pachuco* character in *Zoot Suit*, in the words of Luis Valdez, is "raw, terrible and disgusting to some and glorious to others."[17] El Pachuco is sometimes a negative impulse for Henry, leading him towards violence and misspent pride, such as those moments in prison where El Pachuco coaxes Henry to beat up the guard causing him to be sent to solitary. El Pachuco is also the one shown killing his Chicano brother. But, on the other hand, in the face of racism, El Pachuco is clearly invincible and justified in his rebellion. This is shown in the trial scene. At the trial El Pachuco is the teller of undeniable truths and a figure to emulate because he is self-assured and resistant to assimilationist forces. There are clearly tremendous contradictions in his character.

Valdez' *pachuquismo* molds the separatist youth movement into a progressive myth by adding an indigenous facet. The reference to Aztec origins, perhaps not truly part of the *pachuco* consciousness of the time, works on a symbolic level. El Pachuco is an archetype, as the film says, "a marijuana dream." Henry Reyna as a real *pachuco* confronts the forgotten aboriginal elements of his identity represented by his *pachuco* conciousness. By making analogies between Aztlán and *pachuquismo*, Valdez creates a progressive myth which explains the heroes of the past in terms of their historical significance and connectedness to present political agendas. The film asserts that the Chicano people were able to survive a difficult battle against racism because of this subconscious indigenous identity.

Nevertheless, there remains another fundamental contradiction with the practice of assimilating the *Pachuco* Movement into the Aztec mythology of the Chicano nationalists. Marcos Sánchez-Tranquilino argues:

> The Chicano nationalist movement that began in the 1960s was centrally an antiracist, civil rights movement that rejected all previous identities and defined Mexican Americans as a regionally diversified, multicultural and mixed race people from whom would arise *La Nueva Raza*. Nevertheless, its attempt to shape a politics of unification and nationhood on the basis of reclamation of the indigenous, nonwhite, family-based identity and culture—a Bronze People with a Bronze Culture—suppressed differences and conflicts in the historically antagonistic elements it sought to merge, and remained haunted by a duality of assimilation and secession that the *pachuca* and *pachuco* had already gone beyond.[18]

Sánchez-Tranquilino explains, "*pachuco* culture was an assemblage . . . a cultural affirmation, not by nostalgic return to an imaginary original wholeness and past, but by appropriation, transgression . . ."[19] He describes a discursive space mapped out by *pachuquismo* "between the dualities of rural and urban, Eastside and Westside, Mexican and American and arguably feminine and masculine. Not *mestizo*—half and half—but an even greater *mestizaje* . . . a new space: a new field of identity."[20]

The potential dangers of representing nationalist militancy through the articulation of the *pachuco* are for Sánchez-Tranquilino similar to those which occur in all nationalisms. Their own essentializing of a dominant narrative of a dominant frame of differentiation leads to a static view of culture. The dynamics of gender, class, age, and other elements of personality formation can be stifled. Genero M. Padilla concurs with this observation noting that nationalist myths can sometimes lead to self-delusion and indignant refusal of all criticism. Padilla however, believes nationalist myth can be used as an effective political tool if a certain approach is taken:

> Instead of evaporating into an idealized vision of the past, myth becomes socially powerful at the point where it intersects with history to provide a vision of the future which can be acted upon. The symbol of Aztlán as a mythic homeland provides a field of signs, some actual fragments from the cultural past reinvested with imaginative life, some images altogether invented for the psychic needs of a threatened culture, the interpretation of which may lead the Chicano out of the labyrinth of history into a future neither premised upon delusive fabulations of the past nor bled of the mythic capacity to sustain the story of the cultural self.[21]

In *Zoot Suit*, Valdez avoided promoting a static nationalism by conforming his project to a dynamic view of myth. He took the specific historical moment of *pachuco* resistance during World War II and reinterpreted it through both the myth of Aztlán and a symbolic *pachuco* anti-hero. The dialectical relationship between myth and history found in *Zoot Suit* is redoubled when one considers that some Chicano members of the audience may regard themselves as contemporary *pachucos* through their association with the low rider cultural movement.[22] As El Pachuco relates to this present reality, *pachuquismo* adopts a shifting definition of identity. Similarly, the ambiguous relationship between Henry and El Pachuco can be read as a metaphor for *pachuquismo* as a transformative identity. This interpretation sheds light on Valdez's own reading of El Pachuco, "He represents the essence of what *pachuquismo* is all about . . . this struggle for identity."[23]

THE AMERICAN DREAM AL ESTILO CHICANO: *LA BAMBA* AND LEGEND CREATION

In *La Bamba*, Luis Valdez again deals with myth/legend creation as a frame for Chicano identity, but this time he works within a more traditional structure—the Hollywood musical biopic film. This was Valdez's first venture into genre filmmaking and, as such, provides an interesting example of the problems that can occur when a committed filmmaker interfaces with the genre system.[24] In her study of *La Bamba*, *The Buddy Holly Story*, and *Sweet Dream* (the story of Patsy

Cline), Cynthia Hanson analyzes the way the musical biopic structures the presentation of its protagonist. Hanson observes that the musical biopic chronicles the real life details of a musician's rise from amateur performer to star legend status through a series of scenes designed to emphasize the extraordinary nature of the performer's abilities, By magnifying the uniqueness of the performer's talents, the gap between the performer and the audience is widened. "Stardom," says Hanson, "is by definition distanced from the average."[25]

In *La Bamba*, the rock 'n roll protagonist, Ritchie Valenzuela's rise to stardom and regression from the mean starts when he is "discovered" by a white record producer. Ritchie is performing in a rented Masonic lodge in his neighborhood. The producer shows up looking for talent and later goes to Ritchie's house to persuade Ritchie to come to a basement studio to record a demo. Ritchie shows up, but refuses to sing when he finds out that the producer doesn't want to include the other band members on the record. Forced to make a choice, Ritchie decides "his music" comes before everything else (including his loyalty to the rest of his band) and agrees to do the record. These scenes lead us to attribute Ritchie's break into the music world to a mixture of ingenuity (his mother's idea to rent the hall and "put on a show") and destiny. The scene plays into the ideological underpinning of the biopic genre—that if you have talent and are willing to work hard, you will be discovered.

Ritchie's right to legendary status is further validated in scenes which counterpoint Ritchie's success against his brother Bob's failure. Bob is a frustrated *pachuco* ex-con whose abilities include playing the drums and drawing cartoon characters. At one point in the film, Bob wins free art lessons in an art contest. But this accomplishment is overshadowed by the subsequent announcement of a big record contract for Ritchie. This scene falls right into line with the genre convention. Hanson comments, "Bob serves as a reflection of Ritchie, much like the character of Salieri in Amadeus; focusing on the average person's failed attempts to achieve the success of the performer."[26] The scene magnifies the uniqueness of Ritchie the star and helps establish the required distance between Ritchie and the audience. As the genre prescribes, the scene reminds us, that in terms of stardom, we the audience are more like Bob.

Hanson asserts that in musical biopics, the audience can fashion a relationship with the performer that appears to be participatory. This observation leads her to conclude that there is a regression in the status of the musical biopic's hero from star to average member of the community when the unique talent is blunted through death. The distance between performer and audience at that point in the film is collapsed. She maintains that such is the case in the film *La Bamba* and argues that the audience leaves relating to Ritchie as an average guy not as legend/hero. There is, however, ample evidence to support a contrary reading of the ending of *La Bamba*. I agree with Hansen that the scene when Ritchie's mother hears about his death is sobering, but the sequences which follow, especially the reprise of "La Bamba" at the end, encourage a timeless view of Ritchie as superhuman, as transcendent rock 'n roll myth.

Valdez' obsessive foreshadowing of Ritchie's death works to immortalize the young star. Through the opening dream sequence of the fiery plane crash and continued references to his fear of flying, Valdez parallels the Christian myth of sacrifice (a myth that also informed several of the *mitos* plays by Valdez) casting Ritchie as a hero who is plagued by the ominous specter of his own tragic end. In *La Bamba*, unlike other films of this genre, Ritchie must confront his own mortality to serve a greater cause (his music). Valdez has reworked the generic codes of the musical biopic. Rather than leveling Ritchie's stature through the ending, Valdez elevates the Chicano rocker.

HOLLYWOOD, MYTH AND ETHNICITY

In interviews Valdez gave on *La Bamba*, he reiterated that he was trying to make an "American movie."[27] This statement probably came as no surprise to Chicano activists and cultural critics. Valdez had been discouraging them from misinterpreting his work as ethnic nationalist ever since the *mitos* when he first adopted his neo-Mayan mythic vision. But even his most adamant assertions cannot erase the political contradiction between the use of mythic characters in his films and Valdez's own aesthetic opinions. Genero Padilla explains this problematic in Valdez's theater work:

> How could a drama that proceeded from a nativist orientation, that is, from a desire to restore an ethnocentrically indigenous consciousness, simultaneously

eschew ethnicity and nationalism? The cultural nationalist
argument (with Valdez) hinged on what appeared to be
Valdez's betrayal of the vital objective of cultural
maintenance, namely, the reaffirmation of ethnicity. For
those on the left, Valdez had simply turned his back on
history when he slipped into his cosmic robes.[28]

This same skepticism in regards to Valdez's ultimate objectives bears
consideration in light of *La Bamba*. There are elements in the film that
support an assimilationist reading of the main character, Ritchie. For
instance, Lou Diamond Phillips, who plays the lead, is not of Chicano
ancestry. Also in the film, assimilationist elements of Ritchie's
character are not challenged. He cannot speak Spanish, has never been
to Mexico, goes to a nice middle-class high school and falls in love
with an Anglo girl named Donna. The Ritchie character readily changes
his name from Valenzuela to Valens to further his recording career. He
fits into the white mainstream quite easily and is rewarded for his
talents by a very appreciative American public. These factors contribute
to a reading of Ritchie as the quintessential rags to riches
assimilationist.

But while acknowledging Ritchie's assimilation, Valdez consistently
manages to make ethnicity one of the principal organizing discourses
in the movie. One way he does this is through scenes in which Ritchie
travels across the border to Mexico. In the first Mexican scene, Ritchie
happens upon a traditional *norteña* group playing *La Bamba*. Valdez
makes the point that significant elements of Ritchie's musical roots and
personal spirit come from his Mexican heritage. In the following scene,
Bob takes Ritchie to a *curandero* (healer or shaman). The old native
man berates Ritchie for not knowing Spanish and then gives him an
indigenous snake charm to cure his nightmares. Ritchie wears the
charm, gaining great spiritual comfort from it. He does not remove it
until the end of the film when he goes on his final tour and dies in the
crash. Through very explicit cross cutting, Valdez links the crash to
Ritchie's failure to wear the charm. This validates the power of the
curandero and reaffirms the importance of an indigenous belief system
in Chicano culture. The charm which Ritchie continues to wear
throughout the film serves as a visual reminder of Ritchie's ethnic
heritage.[29]

La Bamba also foregrounds issues of ethnicity through its
presentation of the family or *la familia*. A social concept that was

central in the writings of the Chicano Movement *la familia* was a term used to describe the network of loved ones utilized by Chicanos as a support system. Expressed through the sentiments and actions of Chicano people placing the good of their families and, by extension, their entire community, above their own individual material needs, this concept signified that all Chicanos are *carnales* (brothers of the same flesh and blood), because they shared a common accent, a common alienation, a common experience of being oppressed.[30] The concept of *la familia*, with its attendant emphasis on brotherhood and respect, grew to be accepted by many in the Chicano Movement as having great importance for solidarity building.

The discourse on *la familia* is given considerable weight in *La Bamba*. Valdez shows Ritchie's attachment to his mother to be especially strong. During each step in his career, Ritchie shares his joy with her. The bond is also very tight between Ritchie and his half-brother Bob. Their relationship is, however, troubled because Bob is jealous over Ritchie's success. They come to blows at points, yet, they reconcile just hours before Ritchie's plane crashes as both brothers realize that they need their mutual love to survive.

It is through Bob's character that ethnicity becomes an overreaching theme in *La Bamba*. Bob, the bad brother, has forsaken a vital element of his ethnic heritage—his respect for *la familia*. He is abusive and violent towards his wife. He insults his mother and fights with his brother. His negative behavior is explained in the film by the fact that Bob has not had a father figure in his life. It is further implied that their mother does not love Bob as much as she cares for Ritchie. This dysfunctional family situation extends into Bob's association with society. While Ritchie fits in, Bob is branded an outcast. He has some skill as a cartoonist, but the film shows that, unlike Ritchie, Bob is too ethnic to ever make it in the white dominated world. In sharp contrast to Ritchie's character, Bob's English is accented. His skin is dark. He has a prison record, a *pachuco* tattoo (a cross with three marks) and makes his money running drugs across the border with his gang. Thus, Valdez attributes Bob's marginalization to a combination of racism and the degeneration of the Chicano family structure.

It is precisely the discourse on ethnicity which makes Bob's character more multifaceted and interesting than the one-dimensional character of Ritchie. Bob is the one person in the film who clings passionately to his heritage. He speaks Spanish and encourages Ritchie to learn the language. Bob is also the one who tells Ritchie not to anglicize his surname and introduces Ritchie to Mexico and the ways of the *curandero*. By showing the contradiction between Bob's contented personality when he is with the Indian *curandero* and his dysfunctional personality on the other side of the border, Valdez makes a subtle comment on the problematic relationship between Chicano culture and the American Dream, thereby foregrounding the ethnic issues he set out to avoid.[31]

ETHNICITY AND ETHNIC HEROISM

Although there are important ethnic traits brought out in Ritchie's persona, the ethnic elements of Ritchie's character are ancillary to his construction as a hero figure. Two factors in *La Bamba* lead one to read Ritchie's character as more of an American legend than an ethnic one. The first is a structural limitation imposed by the demands of the genre film. Star biographies tend to reinforce the status quo by creating the illusion that opportunity is meted out fairly according to ability, dedication and hard work. The big break comes to those who deserve it. At the same time, these biopic films affirm a melting pot view of American culture, masking factors such as racial and gender discrimination. Biopics of Al Jolson (*The Jolson Story*, 1946), and Prince (*Purple Rain*, 1984) are examples of ethnic success stories in which the individual performer "transcends" his ethnic roots to become accepted and beloved by the American public. With the Ritchie Valens plot line in *La Bamba* Valdez has chosen to stay within the traditional ideological confines of the genre's view of the ethnic success story. Ritchie, like Jolson and Prince, is presented as possessing unique talent. Thus Ritchie Valenzuela's story line in *La Bamba* feeds into a typical consensus music myth. The myth is based on the idea that music can overcome all boundaries—racial, national, ethnic, sexual, etc. The togetherness mystique attached to Woodstock or the "We are the World" video are examples of this. The notion of the power of music to unify peoples can be found in *La Bamba* during the scene where Ritchie first plays the song "La Bamba" on stage and is enthusiastically accepted by a sea of fawning white girls. Ritchie functions here as the bearer of Mexican folk music as a cultural gift to American youth. The scene feeds into the melting pot myth and fails to adequately question the ethnocentrism of the music business which encourages the public to buy "La Bamba" while at the same time forces Ritchie to change his name. Instead of confronting these issues, the film shows Ritchie's compromises as harmless and inconsequential in the vast scheme of his success.

In the process of taking a Chicano character and transforming him into a mythic rock 'n roll hero, ethnicity is relegated to the level of motif, ultimately having little to do with the thrust of the hero narrative. *La Bamba* is ultimately the story of how Ritchie transcends his ethnicity (embodied in Bob) to join the ranks of open-minded American teenagers. Unlike in *Zoot Suit*, where Valdez unfolds his hero in the cloak of a Chicano myth, (a politicized *pachuquismo*), *La Bamba* is organized by the anglicized "American" music consensus myth. In the end, Ritchie turns out to be an American hero who happens to be a Chicano.

Through Ritchie's character ethnicity is affirmed in a uniquely American way; that is by its value as a potential commodity. Ritchie's talent is his ability to transform the precious gems of his particular cultural heritage into a transnational American art form—rock 'n roll. Thus Ritchie's greatness comes when he rewrites "La Bamba" into a piece suitable for mass consumption. In a similar manner, through the song "Donna," the pain that he feels at being kept away from his white girlfriend by her racist parents is translated into a ballad that goes to the top of the charts. His ethnicity gives Ritchie a unique perspective which he can capitalize on with an American audience. It is his talent as a cultural translator, not his cultural experiences/identity in themselves that justifies our recognition of him as a hero.

CONCLUSION

Zoot Suit and *La Bamba* serve as two examples of how a Chicano director has used narrative film to create popular Chicano heroes through myth. In each case, Valdez developed a hybrid process of retrieving suppressed traditions and inventing new ones. In both films, Valdez establishes linkages with the protagonist and an indigenous Aztec heritage as a source of identification for Chicano viewers.

Valdez created a mythological *pachuco* character in *Zoot Suit* which escaped problems of overromanticizing historical realities by showing how the traditions of the past relate to the conditions of the present. He also avoided the nationalist aesthetic strictures by producing a complex, controversial tragic-hero that problematizes the static nationalist Aztec/Urban warrior figure popularized in other Chicano art forms. The story of El Pachuco is the mythology of an identity in process. Caught between multiple cultures, the *pachuco* myth proposes a cynical identity which interrogates its own precarious autonomy as well.

After years of cultural work, Valdez shows in *Zoot Suit*, that he senses that Chicano ethnicity gains its uniqueness, not by harking back to a homeland, but, rather, through a discourse of interrogation. In *Zoot Suit*, El Pachuco challenges our very notion of heroism by showing the ugly side of *machismo* (his treatment of Alice confines both male and female) and the tragic consequences of individualism and extreme separatism (violence, murder and alienation). By setting up a *pachuco* myth which both sustains and sabotages the protagonist, Valdez approaches, in El Pachuco, Terry Eagleton's definition of the authentic revolutionary subjects created by Brecht and Joyce:

> One of the central political insights of Joyce and Brecht (was) that the political change which matters is not one which recycles the past heroism into the present, but one which undoes all heroism and all manhood.[32]

Zoot Suit's nontraditional narrative deconstructs both Anglo and Chicano stereotypes of heroes and villains, abolishing boundaries typically found in genre films. Just as Sánchez-Tranquilino suggested that *pachuquismo* represented a break from the past, "a new *mestizaje*," El Pachuco represents a break from a nationalist myth structure and, in its place, a new kind of ethnic legend making.

La Bamba, on the other hand, privileges the dominant genre plot embodied in Ritchie's story over a Chicano subplot developed through Bob dramatic line. The mainstream hero, Ritchie Valens, poses no challenge to the hegemony of the Hollywood film industry. References to neoindigenous cosmology become incidental, losing their historical specificity, relinquishing their potential for analysis of current history. Although Ritchie, the hero, is Chicano, his story does not foreground the Chicano mythos in the narrative.

Genero Padilla has pointed out that one of the great errors of the Chicano Movement was not combining a class based analysis with cultural production (myth or otherwise). Valdez has said he was particularly interested in the Valens story because he wanted to deal with working class America.[33] Unfortunately, even though he shows Ritchie as part of the underclass, (through the mise-en-scene of migrant work camps and *barrio* life) Valdez fails to offer an analysis of the class structure in America. *La Bamba* feeds into the American Dream myth inherent in the musical biopic genre by privileging Ritchie's story over Bob's. Also by posing the lack of a father figure as an excuse for Bob's problems, *La Bamba* ignores ethnic and class based oppression as a force which shaped Chicano reality at the time. By not presenting an alternative analysis of the success story on a more overt level, *La Bamba* could easily be seen as contributing to one of the effects of capitalist media on general audiences; to sanitize ethnicity and rid it of its potential for resistance.

NOTES

1. Luis Valdez y El Teatro Campesino, *Actos* (San Juan Bautista, California: Cucaracha Publications, 1971), p. 9.

2. Ricardo Romo and Raymund Paredes, eds., *New Directions in Chicano Scholarship* (La Jolla, California: University of California Press), p. 84.

3. Luis Leal, "In Search of Aztlán," *Denver Quarterly* 16 (Fall 1981): 6.

4. *Documents of the Chicano Struggle* (New York: Pathfinder Press, 1971).

5. Michael Pina, "The Archaic, Historical and Mythicized Dimensions of Aztlán," in *Aztlán: Essays on the Chicano Homeland*, eds. Rudolfo Anaya and Francisco Lomelí (Albuquerque: Academia/El Norte Publications, 1989), p. 35.

6. Ibid., p. 37.

7. José Vasconcelos, "The Race Problem in Latin America," in *Introduction to Chicano Studies*, eds. Livie Isauro Duran and H. Russell Bernard (NY: Macmillan, 1973), pp. 5-27.

8. Jorge Huerta, *Chicano Theater: Themes and Forms*, p. 201.

9. Bill Nichols, *Ideology and the Image: Social Presentation in the Cinema and Other Media* (Bloomington: Indiana University Press, 1981), p. 76.

10. Gaylyn Studlar and David Desser, "Never Having to Say You're Sorry: Rambo's Rewriting of the Vietnam War," *Film Quarterly* 42 (1988): 9-16.

11. During World War II large numbers of servicemen were on furlough in Los Angeles. They would often engage in indiscriminate attacks on Chicanos, especially against those dressed in zoot suits. These attacks escalated into full fledged riots during the week of June 3, 1943 when thousands of servicemen and white civilians stormed East Los Angeles terrorizing Chicanos in their own community. The local police did little to stop the rioting, and several city newspapers applauded the brutality. See Mauricio Mazón, *The Zoot-Suit Riots: The Psychology of Symbolic Annihilation* (Austin: University of Texas Press, 1984).

12. Kathleen Newman notes that self-sacrifice has been an overriding theme in the mainstream media's coverage of Edward James Olmos's performance in *Stand and Deliver*. She suggests this coverage had the effect of neutralizing the subversive tendencies of Olmos's work. Kathleen Newman, "Latino Sacrifice in the Discourse of Citizenship: Acting against the Mainstream, 1985-1988," in *Chicanos and Film* ed. Chon Noriega (New York: Garland Publishing, 1992), pp. 59-73.

13. Rafael Granjeda, "The Pachuco in Chicano Poetry: The Process of Legend-Creation," *Revista Chicana-Riquena* 7, (Otoño 1980): 45-60.

14. Don Porath, "Chicanos and Existentialism," *De Colores* 1, (Spring 1974): 15.

15. Franz Fanon, *Wretched of the Earth*, trans. Constance Farrington (New York: Grove Press, 1963), p. 225.

16. Ibid., p. 240.

17. Oroña-Córdova, "*Zoot Suit* and the Pachuco Phenomenon," p. 99.

18. Marcos Sánchez-Tranquilino and John Tagg, "The Pachuco's Flayed Hide: The Museum, Identity and Buenas Garras," unpublished manuscript of a lecture given at conference entitled "Cultural Studies Now and In the Future," University of Illinois at Champaign-Urbana, April 5, 1990, pp. 16-17.

19. Ibid., p. 8.

20. Ibid., p. 10.

21. Genero Padilla, "Myth and Comparative Cultural Nationalism: The Ideological Uses of Aztlán," in *Aztlán: Essays on the Chicano Homeland*, eds. Rudolfo Anaya and Francisco Lomelí (Albuquerque: Academia/El Norte Publications, 1989), p. 131.

22. For further explanation of the significance of the low rider movement to Chicano cultural studies see chapter 2.

23. Oroña-Córdova, "Interview with Luis Valdez," p. 102.

24. The film did well in mainstream markets, grossing over sixty million dollars at the box office.

25. Cynthia Hanson, "The Hollywood Musical Biopic and the Regressive Performer," *Wide Angle* 10 (Fall 1988): 5.

26. Ibid., p. 20.

27. Gerald C. Lubenow, "Putting the Border Onstage," *Newsweek*, 4 May 1987, p. 79.

28. Padilla, "Myth and Comparative Cultural Nationalism," p. 123.

29. Charles Ramírez Berg reads the plane crash scene as a possible sign of retribution on the part of Valdez for Ritchie's blind assimilationism. Refer to Ramírez Berg, "Stereotyping in Films in General and of the Hispanic in Particular," pp. 286-300.

30. For an in depth discussion of *la familia* and the Chicano Movement refer to Jose Armas, "La Familia de la Raza," *De Colores* 3 (Fall 1976): 35-53.

31. Valdez assumes a patriarchal construction of the Chicano family. He presupposes that a *normal* Chicano family must have a father to serve as a role model.

32. Terry Eagleton, "Marxism and the Past," *Salmagundi* 68/69 (Fall/Winter 1985-1986): 289.

33. Susan Linfield, "Close Up: Luis Valdez," *American Film* (July/August 1987): 15.

IV

BORDER DISCOURSE: STRUCTURING ETHNICITY IN FOUR CHICANO FILMS

INTRODUCTION

The conquest of northern Mexico by the United States in 1848 initiated a massive migration of Anglos to the Southwest.[1] The new population influx quickly and significantly altered the experience of all Mexican and Native Americans living along the border. Lands were taken, houses were burned and resisters were lynched. Spanish and Native languages became markers of otherness. But, in spite of the genocidal policies perpetrated against the population, a cross pollination came about, and a new culture was born in the region; a mix of Anglo, European, African, Asian, Mexican and Native heritages.[2]

Today, the culture of the Southwest has become the focus of and impetus for an avant garde art movement led by Chicanos. Termed "Border Art," it can be described as the "inclusive" expression of Chicano culture and experience. The border arts generated by the Movement avoids essentialism, expressing identity as a multiplicity of subject positionings in and out of the United States. The Southwest has become a fertile sight of cultural interchange, bringing together artists from a variety of ethnic backgrounds. Their styles and experiences converge at the border. They draw much of their inspiration from Chicano art, especially the public arts that emerged during the sixties. Works of border art include murals by painters such as Judy Baca and Willie Herón. Several of these projects cover acres of urban concrete, depicting a politicized Mexican and Chicano consciousness. Other art is inspired by the silk-screened posters of Rupert García decrying injustice and assassination in the *barrios*. The controversial performance pieces by ASCO, a Los Angeles based guerilla theater collective (such as their act of spray painting graffiti on the walls of the Los Angeles Museum of Art) bring issues of institutional discrimination forward for public scrutiny.[3] In the field of the fine arts, the work of David Avalos combines a university training with a popular sensibility, using regional customs for content in his work.[4] Music is also a rich source of expression in the Border Arts. Tex-Mex, a particular Chicano brand of Mexican *conjunto* music, is an example of border art which reaches an international audience via Spanish language radio and television broadcasts.[5]

Guillermo Gómez-Peña is one of the best known border artists and a founding member of the Border Arts Workshop. He started working in San Diego with a group of Chicanos, *Mexicanos* and Anglo Americans who wanted to use art to respond critically to conditions in the border region. Their early work focused on the ongoing human rights violations perpetrated by the Border Patrol and the San Diego Police against Mexican migrant workers. They published *La Línea Quebrada*, a journal containing numerous manifestos critiquing media that justified racist human rights abuses against migrants. In one article, Workshop member Emily Hicks explained three distinguishing features of the border region which influenced the artistic practices of the Workshop:

> 1) deterritorialization (physical, linguistic, cultural, political; 2) the connection of the individual to political immediacy (the inhabitant of the border does not have a self-determined "subjectivity" in the traditional European sense but rather is asked for I.D./refused medical service/threatened with deportation and directly affected economically and politically by Mexico-US relations; 3) the collective assemblage of enunciation: everything takes on a collective value. When one leaves her or his country or place of origin, everyday life changes. The objects which continually remind one of the past are gone. Nostalgia, or reterritorialization, begins.[6]

The reterritorialization or "deterritorialization" that occurs in the process of migration is an operative metaphor for Border Art. For the

Workshop and other border artists, both immigration and emigration are concepts that evoke a notion of crossing more than geographical borders. Migration calls up the idea of transgressing a limitless number of borders. According to Gómez-Peña, the culmination of border crossing is a dynamic intercultural dialogue which pushes cultural/political distinctions and commonalities to their critical mass.[7] The Workshop generated projects which tended to search for new socio-political and artistic ground upon which to initiate a utopian type of intercultural dialogue. Artists in the workshop experimented with a variety of mediums. Gómez-Peña became best known for his performance pieces which served as conceptual investigations commenting on border culture phenomena such as ritual, consumerism, racism and multiculturalism. Yet as the border renaissance appeared to be at its height, Guillermo Gómez-Peña, one of its most celebrated artists, published a controversial article pronouncing the entire Border Arts Movement dead. In his eulogy, Gómez-Peña argued that the Border Arts Movement had reached an impasse because the border as a metaphor had become hollow.[8] He claims this happened because of the "Latino boom" that occurred around 1988. The national media and art institutions "discovered" and embraced border art as an exotic fad. Suddenly border art became grantable and trendy. According to Gómez-Peña, a number of mediocre artists (who he does not name) began imitating the work of artists like David Avalos, James Luna and Gómez-Peña. Eventually the original members of the Workshop were relegated to a peripheral role in the institutionalization of Border Art. Anglo controlled museums and galleries like the San Diego Museum of Contemporary Art, says Gómez-Peña "appropriated, controlled, and presented" Border Art from an Anglicized patriarchal perspective.[9] Art institutions which promoted a few celebrity Chicano artists gradually commercialized work to the point where the art was imitated by those who had no real stake in the border. Upset with this state of affairs, all but one of the original members of the Border Arts Workshop (the only white male of the group) resigned. Gómez-Peña implied that as a result of this process of legitimation and promotion by the mainstream, the original social commitment and multicultural authenticity of the Border Arts Workshop has been lost and cannot be regained by other artists.

Gómez-Peña's complaints about the assimilationist pressures of Anglo art institutions are valid, but he goes too far in dismissing the border as a viable progressive metaphor. One can argue that the border as metaphor has not been totally coopted. Border art is a broader movement with a history that goes back farther than Gómez-Peña has defined it. Uniquely Chicano art has been generated at the border for centuries. The Border Arts Workshop can better be understood as a phase in this long process of hybrid creation. As such, I would argue that the films discussed in this chapter are not part of a so-called bankrupt Border Arts Movement. They are very much invested in the geopolitical discourse that Gómez-Peña and others have so effectively articulated.

As a body of work, Chicano films can be seen as making a significant contribution to the Border Arts Movement. *Break of Dawn*, written and directed by Isaac Artenstein who was, himself, a member of the Border Arts Workshop, develops the theme of cultural self-expression among Spanish speaking people of the southwest. *Raíces de sangre* focuses on the border from the perspective of an international labor movement of Chicano and Mexican workers. *El Norte* articulates a discourse on indigenism and cultural distinctions within a broader Pan-Latin American community. *Born in East L.A.* employs a Chicano aesthetic technique known as *el rasquachismo* to present the story of the political awakening of its Chicano protagonist to issues which affect people in the border region. The analysis which follows will show how the filmmakers extended their own border aesthetic to the feature film format without the use of hollow metaphors or by collapsing cultural identity into cliché.

BREAK OF DAWN

Break of Dawn (1988) is an independently financed low budget film distributed by Director Isaac Artenstein and Producer Jude Pauline Eberhardt through their company Cine West Productions. The film is an expanded narrative version of Artenstein's biographical documentary *Ballad of an Unsung Hero* (1983) about Pedro J. González, a Mexican immigrant, who hosted and produced one of the first major Spanish-language radio programs in the U.S. The film's director, Isaac Artenstein, also born in Mexico, grew up in Southern California and completed a degree in filmmaking at UCLA. He was one of the original members of the Border Arts Workshop where he collaborated with Guillermo Gómez-Peña to produce *Border Brujo* (1990), a video documentation of Gómez-Peña's performance piece on linguistic identity and cross-cultural perception. *Break of Dawn*, Artenstein's first feature, echoes the Border Arts Workshop's preoccupation with the importance of language as a marker of cultural identity and site of resistance. Through his use of historical narrative, issues of linguistic self-determination become enmeshed with other political questions deriving from the era in which the movie is set and which still have relevance to the Latino community today.

The film opens on a shot of San Quentin prison. The colors in the shot are muted, slightly sepia, suggestive of an historical drama. Titles come up, indicating it is 1938. There is a cut to the interior of the prison. A Mexican man is standing before an Anglo prison warden. The abrasive warden interrogates the prisoner, demanding to know why he wrote letters in "Mexican" for other inmates. After withstanding the many insults from the warden, the prisoner becomes enraged and knocks the warden to the ground with one forceful punch. Guards rush in to restrain the prisoner and carry him off to solitary. During a long tracking shot in which the prisoner is led to his cell, additional titles announce that this is the true story of Pedro González, who grew up in Mexico, served as Villa's personal telegraph operator, and who later immigrated to the U.S. in 1928.

This initial sequence establishes the director's cinematic strategy. He aligns the audience's point of view with that of Pedro González. The viewer interprets González' violent response to the warden as justifiable and is gratified at his decision to endure solitary confinement in order to retain his dignity and his freedom of speech. Such positioning of the audience on the side of the underdog is typical of many contemporary social justice films. However, the protagonist in a large number of Hollywood social justice films is often someone who is unenlightened, who does not acquire social consciousness until after suffering an injustice himself (or herself) or witnessing a series of injustices suffered by his or her oppressed ethnic friends (e.g. *Salvador, Cry Freedom*)[10]. In *Break of Dawn* we have immediate identification with a Mexican immigrant who is already acting according to a conscious identity politics. Thus the audience is invested in this man's story from the outset and interprets the subsequent series of flashbacks from a position of commitment rather than naivete and skepticism as is typical of other social justice films.

Using a basic flashback story structure, setting up the first scene with an act of heroism, and aligning truth with the Spanish speaker are all ways the director carefully conveys the ethnic experience to an uninformed audience. But the effectiveness of this approach has come under fire from Mexican film reviewer Jorge Ayala Blanco who argues that such tight control of the audience's perspective is not necessary, especially if the audience happens to be Latino. Ayala Blanco believes that Artenstein's lack of subtlety alienates some viewers who resent such formalistic didacticism.[11] Yet one could make a strong argument to the contrary. The film's opening scene manages to avoid these problems of cinematic pedagogy by making identification a pleasurable experience for the viewer. The viewer gets the satisfaction of temporarily subverting the evil warden through the opening fight scene where González's first act of rebellion against the warden is to answer him in Spanish. His words are translated for the viewer, but not for the warden so that the viewer (whether Spanish speaking or not) is in on the insult and can identify with the act of self-determination. Knowledge of the translation, indicates a privilege leading to new relations of power in the scene, physically and linguistically.

The use of Spanish language becomes a theme in the film as the story develops through flashback. Pedro González and his wife, María, cross the border where they are waved through at a check point by immigration agents. This scene clashes with expectations for a stereotypical Hollywood image of border immigration, replete with narrow escapes and life threatening chases. González and his wife are welcomed by U.S. authorities, not hunted down at gun point. In a subsequent scene during their journey north, they stop alongside the road. Next to them is a poor white family tending to their overheated car. In Spanish, María offers them water. As the whites rudely refuse her kindness, the audience perceives that it is ignorance of the language on the part of these whites which fuels some of their hatred for the Mexicans.

Later, González and his wife arrive at the home of their cousin's family in East Los Angeles. The conversations between them are bilingual. Each of the characters switches back and forth, at points stumbling to translate, but patiently succeeding in communicating. In one scene where María and Matilde (González' cousin's wife) are hanging laundry in the back yard, they engage in a discussion about their husbands. As they compare opinions, their similar experiences as women and as wives help them to transcend the linguistic limitations. A common horizon of experience based on gender as Mexican and Mexican American women becomes the basis of cultural/linguistic interaction. This emphasis on language is further developed in a pivotal scene in *Break of Dawn* when González listens to the radio and discovers that there is no Spanish radio programming in Los Angeles. After trimming his mustache to appear more "in style" (North American), he goes to the local station and asks to host a radio show. He is quickly turned away by the white station manager and told there is no market for such programming. The film then flashes forward to San Quentin. González is naked, in solitary, drinking water out of the toilet. The juxtaposition between the radio station scene and the prison cell foreshadows that González will have to pay a heavy price for bringing Spanish radio to the community.

The following scenes show that González eventually gets his own show on KMPC. It is an early morning music program called "Los Madrugadores" (The Early Risers' Show) which he performs in and hosts. The show is an immediate success, and González goes on to become an immensely popular Spanish-speaking radio celebrity, reaching listeners all over the Southwest. González' ability to garner a vast Mexican American audience is soon recognized for its political potential. He is approached by an ambitious Mexican American police Captain named Rodríquez who asks him to help with the reelection of the white District Attorney. For doing so, González is rewarded with a letter granting him permanent asylum as a political exile. Later, a prominent Mexican American businessman, Señor Rosales, also requests a favor of González. He asks González to promote his stepdaughter for Queen of the Fiestas Pátrias (the Mexican ethnic festival) in exchange for advertising revenues. González is then courted by a third member of the Mexican middle class, the Mexican Consul, Señor Dávila, who wants to use his radio program to lend support to unionizing Mexican immigrant workers in the United States. González agrees to help Dávila despite threats from the District Attorney and Captain Rodríquez. Eventually, because of his pro-union stance, the District Attorney sets González up on a rape charge, offering him probation if he confesses to the rape he did not commit. González refuses to capitulate and is sent to San Quentin.

THE POLITICS OF LANGUAGE

In *Borderlands/La Frontera: The New Mestiza* Gloria Anzaldúa tells of how she and other Chicanos were forced to take speech classes in college in order to "get rid of our accents."[12] In the same essay, she quotes Ray Gwynn Smith on language rights: "Who is to say that robbing a people of its language is less violent than war?"[13] To many Chicanos who came of age during the Chicano Movement, speaking Spanish was a political act, and, to some, it even became an indicator of being Chicano.[14] Decades later, the use of Spanish in Chicano art and culture continues to signify a quest for Mexican cultural roots which have been threatened by many years of racist U.S. policies put in place since the Treaty of Guadalupe Hidalgo.[15]

Today Spanish language and accent still serve as markers of cultural difference in the United States. Outside the Chicano community these traits identify Chicanos and Mexicans as Others. Within the community, Spanish language and accent indicate the degree of similarity and/or acculturation between Chicanos and Mexicans. Beyond this, speaking Spanish is emblematic of other more extended cultural ties and kinships, representing the bonds with Latin America and the Caribbean, legitimizing a Third World political consciousness on the part of Chicanos. Evidence of this expansion in the scope of ethnic identity to encompass new transnational boundaries can be seen in the increased use of inclusive identifying terms such as Hispanic and Latino among Chicanos.

According to political scientist Felix Padilla, Chicanos expand their identity and position themselves as Latino when merited by the political demands of a particular situation. He also observes that the Latino identity label can only be successfully deployed as a mobilizing agent if it appeals to common sentiments or emotional ties within groups. To guarantee its effectiveness as a means of producing solidarity, Padilla asserts the Spanish language must become a site of collective struggle within the community.[16] *Break of Dawn* appeals to this notion of collective struggle by tying Spanish-language rights to a concrete situation of cultural/linguistic-based oppression and by insinuating this situation into contemporary experience. Artenstein shows that the particular Mexican aspects of González' identity are sometimes subsumed within his broader identity as a Spanish speaker. Therefore, this film not only articulates the Mexican American identity issues relevant to the 1940s but also is suggestive of an overreaching "Latino" identity that has become a platform in the 1980s and 1990s as Latino coalitions transform Spanish language expression into an alternative public discursive space.[17]

The present day English-only movement can be seen, in part, as a backlash against the collective expression of Latino identity.[18] *Break of Dawn* was produced in the late eighties concurrent with major campaigns for English-only regulations and the passage of the Simpson-Rodino Immigration Act.[19] As such, the film can be seen as timely commentary. Teresa Montano and Denis Vigil have argued that the English-only Movement is a right wing attempt to systematically deny millions of Spanish speakers the right to bilingual ballots and bilingual education. They assert that this legislation coupled with other factors of racism, would further diminish the already unequal political and economic status of Latinos in the United States. In essence, English-only aims to wipe out cultural ties between Mexican and other Latino populations.

Informed by this historical framework of oppressive immigration policies and the English-only Movement, the narrative turning point in *Break of Dawn*, the silencing of González and his radio program, represents the symbolic act of silencing an entire Latino culture. Stamping out the radio station signifies the muffling of not only a linguistic group but also an "immigrant" group that suffered a class-based oppression as well. The narrative in *Break of Dawn* skillfully develops a discourse on the connection between language, immigration and working class oppression through several scenes showing prevailing racist attitudes towards Mexican immigration and Spanish language use. The second scene in the film, for instance, introduces us to the L.A. District Attorney who uses immigration as a firebrand for his reelection while he is campaigning before a hall of American war veterans. The strained rhetorical style of the District Attorney's speech ("They have taken all your food") and the mechanized nods of approval on the part of the veterans work as shorthand for "fascist gathering."

While the film is a little heavy handed in its use of the D.A. as a villain who has only one motivation (to further his political career), it still manages to articulate a fairly complex analysis of the problems of immigration and self-determination. This is done, for example, in the scene in which a store is raided. The Immigration and Naturalization Service (INS) deports González' cousin and other patrons of a local store to Mexico. In the next scene, the viewer learns that González' cousin is, in fact, a U.S. citizen and sees the stress the arrest places on his family. Thus the viewer is led to read the deportation incident as indicative of a racist immigration system which targets anyone who merely "looks Mexican." Foreignness is revealed to be a category based on appearances. The D.A.'s deportation rhetoric shown in the earlier campaign scene becomes even more suspect when it is considered in tandem with this later deportation scene.

The INS raid sequence also contrasts well with the scene in which González and his wife freely cross the border. As we witness the violent ejection of previously welcomed guests, we begin to see the hypocrisy in the U.S. immigration policies.[20] Later on, the use of the immigration theme comes out again when González is rewarded with a letter granting him political refugee status for using his radio show to bring out the Mexican vote. The incident is played in a somber, ironic tone, for, earlier in the film, González had proudly spoken about riding with Villa in the Mexican Revolution. To accept status as a political exile from Mexico, the country for which he fought, is a serious compromise for González. The audience reads the compromise as tragically necessary given the rampant deportations exacted upon the Mexican American community.[21] The scene also emphasizes the class/economic factors in immigration which often take precedence over political ones.

The reference to the Mexican Revolution of 1910 in the film merits discussion, especially insofar as the Revolution was of serious concern to politicians and big business interests in the United States. A number of Mexican radicals and liberals such as Ricardo and Enrique Flores Magón, Antonio Villarreal and Juan Sarabia fled to Texas and other cities in the United States to escape persecution from the Díaz government. During their exile in the U.S., these Mexican revolutionaries published radical newspapers and began organizing Mexican and Mexican American workers into labor unions, encouraging the union leaders to move toward greater political activism.[22] The exiled revolutionaries also devised a plan to liberate Mexican and African American peoples in the United States by creating a separate nation within North American.[23] These leftist activities made the U.S. government fearful that Mexican immigrants would ignite a working class revolt which would spread throughout the country. In response, U.S. government officials aggressively pursued these dissidents. In the end, several Mexican radicals (such as the

Magón brothers) were captured as the U.S. Cavalry and the Texas Rangers joined forces with the Mexican government to purge the border.

After the revolution triumphed in Mexico, land reform was implemented and several foreign controlled industries were nationalized.[24] American business interests and the U.S. Ambassador were upset with the anti-imperialist policies of the newly-formed Mexican government. There is substantial evidence that these business interests conspired with Mexican opposition forces to assassinate President Madero in 1913.[25] For many decades after the Mexican Revolution, the U.S. government continued to view their southern neighbor as a threat. This was the case during the presidency of Lázaro Cárdenas (1934-1940) who was heading the Mexican government during the years when *Break of Dawn* takes place. Cárdenas implemented many socialist economic reforms including further expropriation and redistribution of lands to the poor and the nationalization of the oil industry.

For contemporary Chicanos, the Mexican Revolution is often regarded as a source of anti-imperialist inspiration and as a link with a revolutionary tradition. The figures of Villa and Zapata have become folk heroes in Chicano culture.[26] The mention of Villa and the Revolution in *Break of Dawn* evokes all these historical connections. As such the reference might produce a sense of victory and empowerment on the part of a Chicano audience invested in the spirit of the Mexican Revolution. For a Mexican audience, however, a sense of irony might surface when confronted with the film's revolutionary references. Many contemporary Mexicans feel that the ideals of the Revolution have been betrayed by a government which is quick to make deals with U.S. business interests leading to economic exploitation of Mexican workers.

In *Break of Dawn*, the allusion to the Mexican Revolution occupies its most prominent place midway through the film when González, after witnessing an attack on a labor organizing meeting by the D.A.'s thugs, denounces the government's actions and then sings a ballad on the air which is critical of U.S. policy. The scene is done totally in Spanish. It is filmed with many point of view shots from the perspectives of the Mexican Americans who listen in the studio. The song evokes recognition, understanding and a feeling of empowerment on their part. At this point in the film, one senses that the Mexican Revolution has finally spilled over the border. Language usage (Spanish), immigration rights, and labor organizing all congeal around one perspective; Chicano justice.

The anti-racist argument in the film is further solidified as we learn that the suppression of the Spanish language is intended as a means of controlling the working class. This is brought out as the narrative shows that the threats against González come after he uses the station as a voice for the masses of Mexican workers. In one telling scene towards the end of the film, the prosecuting attorney goes to KMPC and asks Pedro's boss if he understands Spanish, warning him that González has been advocating Communism behind his back. This scene advances Artenstein's position on language use and class rebellion by tying the suppression of Spanish language rights to red baiting. It is shown that as González is red baited the risks of maintaining his linguistic integrity become magnified. To speak Spanish is to further mark himself as pro-labor and, therefore, dissident. In the eyes of the English speaking power elite he is a radical because he is not only refusing to buy into their version of the American Dream, he is threatening to dismantle it. The power of the Anglos in the film has been maintained, in large part, by the strength of their ideology. All immigrants are taught that success means to assimilate into the existing cultural and economic system. But by speaking Spanish, González challenges this fundamental belief.

Anzaldúa says, "Wild tongues can't be tamed, they can only be cut out."[27] *Break of Dawn* articulates this position with its ending. After González is imprisoned, his wife (with the help of the Mexican consulate) rallies the Mexican American community to secure his eventual release. In a scene before he walks free, González is shown in his cell playing his guitar and singing a Mexican ballad, an eerie lover's lament. González is shot from outside the cell. The bars, in soft focus, intrude on our view of him; a rather literal metaphor for a voice which cannot be silenced even under official state repression. Later, in the final shot of the film, González is released from San Quentin. Several years have passed. Standing at the gate, he looks up at the sunlight. There is an ambivalent gaze in his eyes. Breaking conventions, there is no reverse shot of his wife or anyone else waiting for him outside the prison. The film simply ends on a freeze frame with titles superimposed, telling us that he was deported to Mexico for many years, and that when he was finally allowed to return, his application for a pardon for his conviction was denied by the U.S.

government. This final shot and title sequence sets up a thought provoking open ending to the story, tying the issue of cultural self-determination to a continuing historical dynamic in the present. The titles let the audience know that González is still alive, yet, to this day, remains unpardoned without a radio show/forum or voice.[28]

In *Break of Dawn* the importance of remembrance and its connection to identity formation are tantamount. The protagonist of the film establishes the link between the Mexican Revolution and Chicano resistance. His character embodies what Teshome Gabriel refers to as the "screening of memory" which enforces and continues meaningful subjectivity begun in the past and extended into the future.[29] Gabriel stresses that this type of preoccupation with history by Third World filmmakers confirms their faith in the value of constant struggle. Such is the case with this film by Artenstein. His decision to make this historical narrative at a time when the English-only legislation and the Simpson-Rodino Immigration Act were being debated shows his commitment to activist filmmaking. By drawing connections between past acts of resistance and present situations Artenstein underscores his own commitment to the notion of agency in Chicano art and to producing a film which is informed by both a linguistic and class-based analysis of history.

RAICES DE SANGRE

Raíces de sangre (1977), written and directed by Jesús Salvador Treviño, is the story of a young Harvard educated Chicano attorney, Carlos Rivera (played by Richard Yniguez), who leaves a position at a prestigious law firm in San Francisco to volunteer at a community center in his hometown, a *barrio* along the Texas border with Mexico. The community center in the town is run by a group of deeply committed and politically astute Chicano activists. The focus of their work is to organize the Mexican and Chicano garment workers on both sides of the border against the corrupt Anglo owned Morris Corporation.

Having lived outside the *barrio* for several years, Carlos is the most politically naive of the group. He engages in a series of confrontations with the activists, including a showdown with his old high school friend Juan. Later, Carlos witnesses Juan's death after Juan is attacked by Morris company thugs. These experiences cause Carlos to rise to a new level of Chicano consciousness and activism. The final scene shows Carlos at the forefront of a march of both Mexican and Chicano workers who have come to the gates of the Morris company to mourn the death of their compañero, Juan. Carlos, having decided to remain in the *barrio*, leads them in a call to unity, chanting, "¡*Viva La Raza Unida*!" (Power to the people united!).

The film is an interesting expansion on what film scholar Chon Noriega and others have referred to as a dominant aesthetic practice in Chicano film; the "aesthetics of *barrio* life."[30] The *barrio* aesthetic can be explained as a preference for images that validate and elaborate on the experience of day to day life in the *barrio*. Generally, this tends to be from a working class perspective. *Raíces de sangre* participates in such an aesthetic and extends it into new territory by situating the narrative in a border *barrio*. It takes us visually back and forth across the *frontera* (border) from Chicano *barrio* to Mexican border town as we follow characters through both the main plot and subplot.

In the main plot, Juan leads us from the *barrio* office, south to the *maquiladora* (US factory characterized by low wages and untaxed corporate profits) where we see the conditions of a garment factory he is trying to organize. The place resembles a sweat shop. It is first shown through a montage of close up detail shots of the women sewing. Following this, the dialogue is done in wider shots, picturing the workers seated at their machines. Deep focus in these shots allows the image to always frame another worker in the background, so that there is a sense of repetitiveness and loss of identity associated with factory work. The visuals underscore one of the central problems posed by the narrative: How will the Chicano activists motivate the workers to break through this anonymity and establish themselves as self-determining subjects?

We are granted a brief vision of their potential for self-actualization as several of the Mexican workers speak of organizing. Román, for example, is the union organizer who works in the shop. He has conversations with several of the women characters about forming a new union with the Chicano workers. Román moves through the space of the factory. His freedom to circulate within the confines of the work area contrasts markedly with the lack of movement by the women who are rarely shown away from their sewing machines. In a later scene, the women are pictured sabotaging the work space. The change in their posture, the act of standing up and walking out is a physical gesture of liberation. As they take over their work place, they regain control of their subjecthood.

Raíces de sangre contains a subplot depicting the life of a Mexican husband and wife who go north in order to find better paying jobs. The wife is a worker in the Morris garment factory. She and her husband have several scenes in their home, a very modest three room space where they live with their three children. These scenes of Mexican working class life make clear the economic pressures which lead the family to emigrate. In the end, the husband and wife perish in the back of a locked truck which is abandoned by the *coyote* after crossing the border.[31] The subplot teaches us that the daily life of the Chicano *barrio* includes the plight of Mexican workers. The *barrio* in this film is a place that transgresses borders and a rich symbol of unity between the Chicano and Mexican people in the face of oppression.

Through the story of Carlos' coming to consciousness, the metaphoric significance of the *barrio* is further enriched. The community center, prophetically named "*Barrio Unido*," is the launching pad for his journey back to his own working class roots. Carlos is the prodigal son, nurtured by the community in hopes that he would return to share his knowledge and skills with his people. Carlos, however, refuses to undertake his duty and to comprehend the daily truths of *barrio* life. Carlos' struggle sets up a discourse on the importance of the *barrio* to Chicano identity. The film shows how separation from the daily life of the *barrio* has hardened Carlos towards his community. He has adopted middle class and, in some respects, assimilationist attitudes towards the problems faced in the daily life of the essentially working class and underclass community. This is brought out very literally. In one telling scene, Carlos verbally attacks Juan for not reporting a drug incident to the police. "When are these *vatos* going to learn," he argues with the activists. Juan answers, "These *vatos* are your problem too," emphasizing the importance of collective responsibility of Chicanos to the *barrio*.

Carlos also lacks the humility expected of a community organizer. There are several scenes which emphasize the distance his new economic status has placed between himself and the community. He callously puts one of the activists down for misspelling the name of the Morris Corporation on a placard, "Before you can fight La Morris, you have to know how to spell it." In another scene, Carlos is

uncomfortable with being around a group of lowriders who are friends
of Juan's. Carlos declines their invitation for a beer and makes an
excuse to avoid them. These scenes of Carlos' distancing are played
very pointedly to underscore how out of place Carlos has become in his
own community. Through constant undercutting of Carlos' bourgeois
attitudes, the scenes essentialize Chicano identity, dictating a definition
of the *barrio* as a working class space.

The discourse on the *barrio* is further developed in scenes which
associate confrontation and revolutionary struggle with the realities of
everyday Chicano life. There is a sequence where all the workers
assemble peacefully in the park to protest the Morris Corporation. The
gathering is violently attacked by police and men hired by Morris. The
struggle is shown for several minutes and includes many shots of the
workers being beaten and trying to fight back. After this scene, there
is an episode in the barrio office which shows the activists holding a
press conference. On the wall, are black and white stills of the
incident. The photographs resemble shots the audience may have seen
published in real newspapers in the sixties and seventies. It recalls the
legacy of police violence against the Movement, especially the killing
of *L.A. Times* journalist, Rubén Salazar and two other Chicanos by
anti-riot police at the Chicano Moratorium, an anti-war rally in August,
1970.[32]

A turning point for Carlos in the film comes when he gains a
revolutionary perspective on the violent *barrio* reality. This happens
while Carlos is at Juan's death bed. In a very melodramatic moment,
Carlos confesses his betrayal of the struggle and promises to give up
his wealthy, privileged lifestyle and return to his roots. But the film
goes on to say that Carlos' change in attitude is not enough. The day
of Juan's wake, Carlos storms into the community center and becomes
enraged that the people of the *barrio* have sent candles to honor the
memory of Juan. Instead, Carlos wants them to take to the streets and
fight. He is enraged at what he considers a passive reaction on the part
of the community to what has happened. The head organizer, Rogelio,
castigates Carlos for this attitude, "*Esto no es un juego de ahorita. Esto
es una lucha para toda la vida.*" (This isn't a game we can win right
now. This is a struggle to be fought over a lifetime.) The lesson, it
seems, is that the revolution must come from the *barrio*, not from a
few individuals. Carlos must learn self-sacrifice and humility. He must
lose his blinding pride and become one with the *barrio*. And this does

happen in the final scene. Carlos takes part in a symbolic communion with his people as he leads them in a funeral procession to the gates of the Morris Corporation. The scene signifies his reunion with his *Raza* and their struggle.

Raíces de sangre posits a view of the border as a sight of revolutionary Chicano consciousness which is not altogether unproblematic. In many respects, the revolutionary work envisioned in the film is romanticized in a very conventional manner. For instance, the *barrio* office is unaffected by egotism or factionalism. Deep personal connections between the staff and the community generate idyllic satisfaction and fulfillment. Only the uncommitted Carlos threatens to disturb the sacred bonds of radical commitment. The office is also a place where gender equality is practiced. The leading female character, Lupe, is treated with respect by her coworkers and seems to have as much power in running the office as her *compañeros* do. But on the level of the visuals, the film objectifies Lupe's character and suffers structurally in respect to its use of the Chicana as a love interest. In the scene when Carlos is first introduced to everyone in the office, Lupe is the only character shown in the close up. She is clearly the subject of Carlos' and the audience's sexually charged gaze. As the male story lines develop, Lupe's place in the narrative is reduced to a love interest for Carlos. The power she potentially commands in the opening of the narrative via her radical consciousness is dissipated each time Treviño cuts to a glossy tight shot of Lupe looking dreamily at Carlos. Her story line climaxes when she makes love with Carlos. Her attraction to Carlos, the least politicized of the organizers, is not presented as a contradiction in the film, nor does the narrative deal with the effect their affair might have on the dynamics of the *barrio* office. In this Chicano revolution, a man can flounder ideologically while still attracting the most committed *compañera* to his bed. While one could argue that this may actually happen in revolutionary movements, in this movie, the failure to articulate the incident as contradiction ignores the true role of the Chicana character in the Movement.

Though *Raíces de sangre* romanticizes revolutionary struggle, its analysis of immigration in the context of international revolution is intensely illuminating. In the film, we are shown a web of corruption that extends between both borders. We are told in the scene where Pepe is talking with his Chicano coworkers outside the plant that the Morris

Corporation and other U.S. companies have used "*mojados*" (wetbacks or migrant workers) to replace Chicanos who threaten to strike. This corporate manipulation is shown as the source of misguided contempt for the Mexican immigrants by the Chicano labor force. On the other side of the border, the Mexican workers, we are told, distrust the Chicanos because they receive slightly higher wages than the laborers in the *maquiladoras.* We see how the two groups are played against each other and how their refusal to unify benefits the Morris Corporation. The mutual distrust escalates into hatred as some of the Mexican workers are paid by Morris to beat up rallying Chicano workers.

Also drawn into the circle of immigration is the opportunistic union leader, Alvarado. He and other establishment union officials are in collusion with the Morris bosses. We find out that Alvarado has even been using Morris trucks to transport migrants north. Through the subplot with the Mexican family, we further learn that it is because of the low wages Morris pays that they must immigrate in the first place. When the couple does finally cross the border, they must pay the *coyote* (who then gives the cash to Alvarado) several hundred dollars. The argument is clear. Treviño shows that immigration at the Mexican border is the result of an oppressive capitalist economic structure which is international in scope. Moreover, Treviño offers a possible solution to this problem; that is, to instigate an international revolutionary struggle fought by the Mexican and Chicano working class.

The leftist vision espoused by Treviño in *Raíces* echoes the anti-imperialist revolutionary teaching coming out of Latin America during the sixties and seventies. Even before the first Chicano film was produced, Luis Valdez traveled to Cuba as part of an international exchange of students through the Progressive Labor Party. After observing the Cuban revolutionary process first hand, he and another student activist created the first radical manifesto to be written by Mexican American students:

> The Mexican in the United States has been . . . no less a victim of American imperialism than his impoverished brothers in Latin America. In the words of the Second Declaration of Havana, tell him of misery, feudal exploitation, illiteracy, starvation wages, and he will tell you that you speak of Texas; tell him of unemployment, the policy of repression against the workers, discrimination

... oppression by the oligarchies, and he will tell you that
you speak of California; tell him of U.S. domination in
Latin America, and he will tell you that he knows that
shark and what he devours, because he has lived in its very
entrails. The history of the American Southwest provides
a brutal panorama of nascent imperialism.[33]

Several years later, Treviño, himself, went to Cuba. In 1978 *Raíces de sangre* was awarded a prize for best script. In 1981, he was invited back to serve as a festival jurist. The anti-imperialist thrust of the New Latin American Cinema Movement generated a degree of Pan-Latin American unity among filmmakers. The works of Freire, Martí and Fanon informed the film manifestoes of the time, giving rise to an anticolonialist struggle that embraced all Latin American peoples.

Latin American film scholar, Ana López, comments on the radical nature of this tendency of the New Latin American Cinema to foster a hemispheric cultural consciousness:

It is in precisely a movement that stresses a particular set
of nationalist positions and that articulates these positions
across a terrain much broader than the national sphere that
the New Latin American Cinema acquires its revolutionary
cultural significance. It does not just represent a national
cultural response to the specific forces of development and
underdevelopment of a particular nation state, but an
attempt to incorporate the importance of the national within
the necessary Pan-Latin American nature of class-cultural
struggle.[34]

Raíces de sangre reflects the shift towards Pan-Latin Americanism in the Chicano Cultural Movement. Chicano consciousness, in this film, is decidedly framed within a working class identity. Moreover, this class identity sees as its enemy, not just white cultural-economic oppressors, but all agents of bourgeois control regardless of ethnicity. Carlos' middle class attitudes and Alvarado's opportunism are equal negative forces that must be purged if the *Raza* can move forward. As is the case with the New Latin American Cinema, *Raíces de sangre* becomes Pan-Latin American by promoting unity against global capitalism as its common enemy. This point is made quite literally in the scene of the protest rally where a Chicano theater production is shown. In the play there is a character called Tío Sam (Uncle Sam), costumed as a pig, dressed in a top hat, holding a big sack. When he is asked by the character of the corporate boss to give him Mexico, Tío Sam reaches into his sack and pulls out a single dollar bill.

THE CHICANO/MEXICAN DIALECTIC

According to José Angel Gutiérrez, there are four major ideological positions on the part of Chicanos with regard to their perceived relationship with Mexico. First, there are those who perceive themselves to be Mexican. A second group sees themselves as a distinct ethnic community separate from both Mexican and United States identities. A third group is comprised of cultural pluralists. This group posits their Mexican ancestry as a more inclusive Third World identity. A fourth group consists of Mexican Americans who view their heritage as more symbolic than formative.[35] The discourse on Mexican/Chicano cultural interrelatedness in *Raíces de sangre* falls within this third ideological camp. The most strident declaration of this position comes as the film names Mexicans and Chicanos under the term *Raza*. Raza, says Francisco Camplís, in his manifesto on Chicano Cinema, is a more embracing term than Chicano or Mexican American. It refers to the Indio-Hispano experiences of the culture in terms of the shared effects of oppression and colonialism:

> Raza, in my opinion, has an international connotation as well as the philosophical and ideological implications ... Raza Cinema could also reach out internationally and form linkages with other Mexicanos and Latin Americans and other Third World oppressed peoples struggling for liberation.[36]

By reading the connections between Mexican and Chicano culture through a broader Third World Raza identity, the film manages to avoid the problem of stereotyping, not only Chicano culture but Mexican culture too. Carlos Monsiváis, in his article, "The Culture of the Frontier: The Mexican Side," has explained how the basic contradiction in Mexican culture along the border continues to be a symptom of a dependent society in which "an apparent cultural nationalism is accompanied by resignation to exploitation."[37] According to Monsiváis, the official bureaucratic Mexican culture repeats old theories of "*raíces,*" that is the safeguarding of traditions, while sanctioning continued invasion by U.S. corporate consumer interests. For the Mexican border citizen, the call to *raíces* or national character has come to signify an anomalous identity: "National character as a once-only marvelous experience, hedged in by the envy and the desire to submit to foreign powers."[38] *Raíces de sangre* shatters the repressive facade of Mexican nationalism by infusing the call to *raíces* with connections to real economic and political border struggle.

It is noteworthy that the film was produced by the national film company of Mexico, CONACINE. Treviño utilized Mexican and Chicano actors and crew for the production. The success of securing the joint venture lead the director to feel, at the time, that the Mexican government would continue to fund coproductions. However, when the Echevarría presidency ended, so did talk of financial assistance to Chicano directors. CONACINE was eventually dismantled. *Raíces de sangre* was distributed in the United States in Spanish through the now defunct Azteca Film distribution company and can be found on the shelves of certain Latino video stores across the United States.

EL NORTE

El Norte (1983) was directed by Gregory Nava and was co-written by Nava and his wife, Anna Thomas, who also served as producer. The story depicts the odyssey of two adolescent Guatemalan Indians who are forced into exile after government death squads raid their village, murder their father and abduct their mother. The protagonists, Rosa and Enrique, Maya-Quiché youth, who have never gone very far from their native town, are forced on a journey north through Mexico to San Diego. Instead of finding the freedom and prosperity they are searching for in the U.S., they are confronted by hardship, isolation and tragedy. The climax of the film comes as Rosa dies in her brother's arms.

The story structure resembles both melodrama and epic. It is epic in its allegorical qualities and in the sense that it is a journey film. *El Norte* is a melodrama in its attention to the personal relations of Rosa and Enrique. The plot resembles a love story with brother and sister desperately fighting against the cultural, political and economic pressures which threaten the deep bonds between them.

El Norte is divided into three acts separated by fades and titles. The first act, called "Arturo Xuncax" is set in a remote Mayan village in the highlands of Guatemala. The protagonist of the sequence is collectively embodied in the extended Mayan family of Enrique and Rosa. *El Norte* constructs this family in utopian terms. Tradition binds the nuclear unit tightly together. The daughter works beside the mother who makes tortillas for the evening meal. At dinner, they are joined by the *padrinos* (godparents) in the quiet warmth of their modest living space. A young man knocks at the window and Rosa respectfully asks her parents' permission to go speak with him. At dusk, the young lovers stroll in the plaza where they are serenaded by the sounds of indigenous music. But the serenity of the native existence is soon disrupted. Arturo, their father and a man of immense dignity, must go meet with the other *campesinos* (peasant farmers) of the village. His son, Enrique, wants to follow, but Arturo tells him to stay home.

Arturo leads a clandestine organizing meeting of coffee pickers in the town, but they are soon ambushed by army death squads. Arturo escapes but is pursued by a sinister looking soldier. Enrique, as if spiritually awakened by his father's endangerment, sits up in bed and then rushes to the plaza to help his father. There Enrique sees the terrible sight of his father's decapitated head hung like an omen in the street. Enrique comes upon the soldier who murdered his father. Enrique kills the soldier and then flees. The next morning the army disappears[39] most of the women in the village, including Rosa and Enrique's mother. Rosa escapes capture by hiding at her godmother's house. After the army leaves, the town seems possessed by foreboding spirits. Rosa sits by the family altar while thousands of white butterflies mysteriously appear. Her brother returns to bury their father. The townspeople, dressed in traditional Mayan clothing, march towards the burial sight. The land is green and lush and scattered with imposing twenty foot white crosses that create a sense of magic and an alternative indigenous mise-en-scene.

Nava has mentioned his intent to reinvent a Latin American "magical realist" style in *El Norte*:

> In Latin America the great writers . . . all of their work
> has a combination of fantasy with the harsh realities of life.
> I felt that the only way to be true to that world and to these

> characters was to bring to the screen the style found in
> novels like *El Señor Presidente* and *One Hundred Years of*
> *Solitude*.[40]

Magical realism is a literary technique which has been used in the works of Asturias, García Marquez and others. Their stories and novels capture the supernatural/mystical elements of Latin American culture, reflecting deep connections to the indigenous heritage of the continent. Reality is filtered through a vision of history which is cyclical, following a pattern that traces a pre-Columbian world view through the conquest into contemporary times and then ultimately towards reestablishment of an indigenous society that joins past and present, completing the circle. Through the course of the story, reality is interpreted through an indigenous world view which provides an outlook on history which combines the mystical with the concrete. An interesting discussion of the genesis of American magical realism (*Lo real maravilloso americano*) can be found in the preface to *El siglo de las luces* by Cuban writer, Alejo Carpentier.[41] There he explains how, in his view, European culture is suffering from fatigue; all its imagination spent over the centuries. Carpentier reasons that we are in an epoch in which the Europeans must rest and the subjugated cultures of Latin America must necessarily rise up and take over. Because there have been generations of mixed races, a constant coming together of cultures, Latin America has and will continue to produce a distinct vision of the world. Carpentier argues that instead of trying to escape reality through art, as many European cultures have done, the Latin American artist accepts reality in new imaginative ways.[42]

The magical realist style is transmitted in *El Norte* through richly colored mise-en-scene, references to Mayan mythology and experimental story structure. The mise-en-scene in the initial episode uses the saturated coloring of a Mayan village, creating an alternative pallet and visual space. The interiors in the town are tropical shades of blues, pinks and reds that reflect the same colors found in the brightly patterned native dress (*huipiles*[43], hand woven smocks) worn by the villagers. Such intensive use of color, however is not found in the next two episodes of the film which are shot in Mexico and the United States. The later chapters of the story belie a much duller palette and, consequently, a much more alienating reality for the protagonists.

The references to Mayan culture are abundant. Lucila Vargas has pointed out that the story of the two siblings whose father is beheaded can also be found in the *Popul Vuh*, the sacred book of the Mayans.[44] Many scenes contain elements of nature that hold symbolic meaning in Guatemalan culture. For example, Vargas notes that there is a scene of a man denouncing Rosa and Enrique. The scene begins with the camera on a *guacamayo* (parrot), an animal which signifies a braggart in the Maya-Quiche tradition. In the third act, Rosa suffers from typhoid and hallucinates that she is reunited with her father who is holding a dead fish in a basket, an omen of death in Mayan culture. The effect of these references is to lend an indigenous layer of meaning to the film; a filter relating reality to the cosmic order of the Mayan empire.

Indigenism played a critical role in the Chicano Cultural Movement. As was discussed the previous chapter, the search for the native "essence" of the Chicano persona led to the adoption of the Atzlán myth which then became one of the most powerful symbols to advance the Movement. While the concept of Indigenism for the Chicano Movement often privileges the native aspect of Chicano identity over other facets, Chicano indigenism is not a theory of racial purity, but has developed into a more complicated notion of *mestizaje* (mixed blood). Such a construction of identity, explains Tomás Ybarra-Frausto, contradicts U.S. concepts of nativism and the strong Calvinist heritage which privileges "purity." To be *mestizo* means to stand in opposition to the mainstream. From a political standpoint, indigenism/*mestizaje* provides a framework for envisioning a collective identity that spans both American continents offering Chicanos a vast social power base in the form of a strong oppositional coalition of native peoples.

However, unlike in other Chicano films, in *El Norte* indigenism is not developed as a political rallying point to unite Latinos. The film is about a specific Mayan ethnic group, not a symbolic heritage as it functions in other Chicano films. Indigenous ethnicity is foregrounded as concrete and local. The director structures the three episodes in *El Norte* to highlight cultural differences among Latinos, creating three distinct identities in the narrative; Mayan, Mexican and Chicano. The journey of Rosa and Enrique is a device for showing these three identities as stages in a process towards greater and greater mixing of ethnicities or *mestizaje*.

Differences between Latinos are underscored by dividing the film into three sections. The first is set in Guatemala, the second in Mexico and, the third, in the United States. This structure emphasizes the borders between the countries as more than physical barriers. Borders are cultural filters where the purity of indigenous life is gradually skimmed away and eventually discarded. Take, for instance, the contrast between the scene where Rosa and Enrique leave Guatemala and the scene in which they appear in Mexico. In Guatemala, Rosa is shown preparing for the exodus. The light is gentle, cutting through holes in the walls of the family shrine. Rosa removes her native dress and puts on western clothing. The scene is enacted with intense gravity and sorrow and implies a spiritual loss. After Rosa puts on the western garb, an ominous wind possesses the village, slamming doors of homes where families have been disappeared. Rosa emerges in her street clothes, not looking like herself. She hurries down a narrow path past two *brujas* (magical women) chanting her name. In the nearby misty mountains, Rosa meets up with Enrique, and the shot fades to black. The next scene bombards us with noise, light and motion of another sort. A freight truck roars through the bright, arid Mexican terrain. Brassy *conjunto* music blares from a radio while a demonstrative Mexican truck driver shouts out a litany of "*de la chingadas*" (Mexican expletives). The juxtaposition of the two cultures through drastic visual and aural contrasts forces us to see distinctions and separations, to recognize Rosa and Enrique as the authenitc indigenous others. The Mexican in this instance is, the *mestizo* and the dominant culture. The Spanish language used by the Mexican truck driver, is, ironically, alien to Rosa and Enrique who favor speaking in their native Maya-Quiché idiom. Whereas in other Chicano films Spanish is coded as a marker of an unproblematic Pan-Latin American identity, in *El Norte* Spanish is the language of the oppressor (the Guatemalan landowner) and the now "foreign" Mexicans and Chicanos.

The disjunction between Latino cultures continues as a motif into the third episode. The sequence begins as Rosa and Enrique are brought by their *coyote* to Don Mote, a Chicano labor broker. Mote is a conniving wall-eyed opportunist. He speaks mostly English. His Spanish is almost nonexistent. He is the last link in a chain of linguistic mutations which, over the course of the film, culminates with Enrique and Rosa studying English in night school. Don Mote also represents the farthest point from the moral codes and traditions of indigenous life. He is purely motivated by greed and profit. He sets himself up as their only contact for employment, then takes most of their low wages by renting them an apartment he owns. In a later scene, Enrique meets another Chicano while working in a posh Los Angeles restaurant as a bus boy. Enrique is promoted to waiter ahead of the Chicano coworker. The Chicano, jealously calls the INS to raid the restaurant. Both Chicanos, Mote and the bus boy, act in self-serving ways. They clearly perceive their Chicano identity as an indicator of difference and superiority over Enrique. They are at the opposite end of the Latino continuum constructed in *El Norte*.

In contrast to the Chicanos, the Mexican characters in this third chapter of *El Norte* are painted in a more favorable light. Both Enrique and Rosa befriend their Mexican coworkers in the United States. Their status as illegals becomes the cohesive force, or the common experience that binds Mayan and Mexican together. Hence, the alienation felt by Rosa and Enrique in the second episode set in Mexico is superseded as they now find themselves bound by class ties to the Mexican "illegals" in opposition to a powerful North American bourgeoisie. Cultural solidarity is shown to be, in part, a process of shifting alliances effected by the economics of immigration.

It seems through the tripartite structure that the director is attempting to present a politicized regional view of immigration and labor exploitation. Unfortunately, the film has several inconsistencies and rhetorical gaps that prevent it from doing this effectively. A major stumbling block with the film is that each of the three chapters is narratively structured like a separate film. Each has a problem posed, a climax and a brief resolution. The effect of the three films within a film structure is to discourage the audience form deriving meaningful connections between the episodes. For instance, the first story poses two plot problems; fighting the rich landowners and the escape from Guatemala. The first plot conflict is dealt with in the narrative by showing it to be insurmountable. Enrique's only option against the power structure becomes escape rather than confrontation. The second plot line, the escape, is resolved as both Enrique and Rosa safely slip out of their village into the cover of the mountains. In the Mexican chapter of the film, the problem of crossing the U.S./Mexican border directs the plot. This comes to a climax when Rosa and Enrique are forced to crawl through a rat infested tunnel. The resolution is achieved as the two stand atop a ridge looking down on the lights of San Diego. In the final episode of the film, the plot shifts once again and the focus of the story becomes the question of whether or not Enrique and Rosa can maintain their traditional Mayan values. The sequence reaches its climax when Enrique must chose between accepting a good job in Chicago or staying with his sister (an anchor for his Mayan identity) in Los Angeles. The plot is resolved by his decision to stay.

Consequently, each chapter in *El Norte* serves as a self-contained parable in the journey of two Mayans away from their roots. This repeated closure discourages a possible radical reading of the last scene in the film which shows Enrique digging a ditch in Los Angeles. In the scene is a shot of his father's head hanging in the village, followed by a cut to a full moon in Guatemala. This ending connects Arturo's pronouncement in the first scene *"para el rico, el pobre solo es brazos"* (for the rich, the poor are only a pair of arms), to Enrique's situation in the United States. He, like his father is the instrument of the rich. But we do not go on to ask why is this so and how can it be changed because the closed parable structure divorces us from drawing meaningful connections between poverty, immigration and imperialist exploitation in the region.

The three separate story structure also shifts our attention away from a more radical understanding of Enrique's plight by changing the bad guy or narrative obstacle that is presented in the first sequence to a different set of problems in the second and third sequences. The rich landowner who is the villain in the first episode is dropped as a character after the first thirty minutes of the film. The Immigration Service takes on the role of bad guy in the remainder of the movie. The Immigration Service's threat short circuits the possibility for openly depicting the causal links between the military threat in Guatemala and Rosa's tragic death from typhus at the end. We see how the two siblings are able to safely cross into Mexico, but when they try to enter the U.S., they must crawl through a rat-infested sewage pipe in order to avoid capture by U.S. authorities. From the rats, Rosa contracts typhus, but she does not seek medical treatment because of fears that she'll be deported. Her death is shown to be caused by restrictive immigration laws not the deeper structural flaws in capitalism.

Within the constraints of the melodrama, the concentration on the lives of the two ghettoized siblings takes on the characteristics of a love story. It saturates us with their devotion and builds suspense by setting up the INS as the ever-present threat to their happiness together. In this way, the story line obscures the initial focus of the tragedy of a family and a pueblo living in constant threat of extermination. *El Norte* opts for a different social message. It tells us we should accept all Latino immigrants because they are warm and hardworking individuals. It also says that these immigrants come to the U.S. because of corruption in their own countries. The act of deportation, therefore is seen as the principal obstruction to the consummation of the platonic love between the siblings. A corollary which the story implies is that hard working men and women like Enrique and Rosa could indeed succeed within this economic system if the menace of deportation was not held over their heads.

What begins as an epic tale of the Mayan people becomes a melodramatic parable of all immigrants who have come from and remain in poverty. Yet, for all the references to poverty, its meaning within the film remains ambiguous. Early on, for instance, Arturo Xuncax tells his son that in their country, the rich own all the good land forcing the poor to work like beasts of burden on that land which they will never own. The film assigns the cause of poverty within Guatemala to evil landowners who are never shown. They are an absent threat, yet they are the only subjects the film blames for the people's poverty. By locating the source of oppression in an overly stereotyped notion of the landowner, the film confuses the issue of economic impoverishment of the Third World and especially does not deal with imperialism. Arturo's emotional speeches are reduced to cliches as the film fails to develop a more complex explanation of poverty within the context of the material conditions of the region.[45] Poverty is coded in *El Norte* as a state of disgrace that has befallen Central America because of internal corruption. The logic of the film leads to a centrist interpretation of the solution. Salvation for the immigrants can be bestowed by letting them enter the U.S. freely, without threat of deportation.

This kind of conflict resolution is safe for North American viewers; it allows for emotional involvement and identification with the impoverished immigrant while never exposing the contradictory position the viewer embodies via his/her U.S. citizenship in a government which backed a right wing military coup in Guatemala and set the entire program of disappearances in motion. Such an approach to poverty promotes an attitude of tolerance. Herbert Marcuse has explained how a tolerant outlook, in fact, is derived from the very causes of oppression:

> The conditions of tolerance are loaded: they are determined
> and defined by the institutional inequality . . . It is of two

> kinds: (1) the passive toleration of entrenched and
> established attitudes and ideas even if their damaging effect
> on man and nature is evident; and (2) the active, official
> tolerance granted to the Right as well as the Left, to
> movements of aggression as well as to movements of
> peace, to the party of hate as to that of humanity . . . in
> doing so it actually protects the already established
> machinery of discrimination.[46]

By couching the story of the Guatemalan immigrant in the emotional cliches of melodrama, toleration and not confrontation becomes the mode of address which the North American viewer is encouraged to adapt. Consequently, the film evokes sympathy, but true understanding of political and economic underpinnings of immigration for Central Americans and their radical alternatives (such as indigenous resistance movements) are avoided.

My analysis presumes an uninformed predominately eurocentric audience for the film. This is because the filmmakers and distributors themselves have indicated that this group was the target market for the film.[47] However, one can see how an alternative reading could emerge from the film, especially on the part of Central American refugees in this country and abroad. For them the film's cliched dialogue and stereotyped situations can work as cues to call up lived experience, which itself may offer the exile a deeper understanding of their oppression. To the refugee, *poverty* and the absent landowner are not ambiguous concepts. By bringing outside information to the film, the exile can supplement the narrative, discard the ideological position of toleration advocated by the text and, in a sense, reread the film as a chronicle of the sufferings of the Central American in general.

Such a reading would also permit an alternative interpretation of the last sequence of the film, a shot of Enrique digging a ditch in the U.S. followed by a flashback to the head of his father hanging form a tree. The scene could be read as a juxtaposition of the son's experience in the U.S. with the father's in Guatemala, as linking the entire system of oppression to the dominant class' economic and political interests in *both* countries. Unfortunately, informed viewing is limited because of the restrictive conventional modes of distribution and consumption.

For the majority of viewers, *El Norte* constructs a patronizing vision of Mayan culture and the problem of poverty. On the one hand, the film valorizes the indigenous lifestyle where the ethos of family and community solidarity are held sacred. The filmmaker consistently gives us scenes pitting an idyllic Mayan culture against a corrupt *mestizo* one. At the same time, the trajectory of the narrative undermines the protagonist's potential as a self-determined indigenous subject. Enrique never speaks of going back home, never contemplates joining a Guatemalan human rights organization or resistance movement either in the U.S. or in Guatemala. Such an action would be a logical step for his character, given that his father tried to start a resistance movement himself.[48] After the brother and sister flee, references to Guatemala are limited to visions of terror (the appearance of the killer "jaguar") and surreal dreams (Rosa's vision of meeting with her father in the garden). Their only option, in terms of the narrative, is to head north towards economic opportunity. Embracing capitalism, not questioning its flaws, becomes an inevitable solution.

This liberal world view is also what eventually influenced decisions by Nava and Thomas when it came time to distribute *El Norte*. The producer and director asked that all allusions to politics be avoided in the marketing campaign:

> We wanted to convey the universal theme and quality of
> the story, not letting people get confused by the political
> associations they might have with the subject matter.[49]

It was agreed that the distributors, Island Films, would limit the movie's use for benefit screenings, "We didn't want the film to appear a political tool and divide the community."[50] When PBS aired *El Norte*, it was also presented as an immigration parable.[51] This strategy to interpret the film as something other than the story of indigenous self-determination was a financially successful one. The movie cost only $850,000 to produce and had grossed over 5.6 million in box office receipts as of 1990.

BORN IN EAST L.A.

The films *Break of Dawn*, *Raíces de sangre*, and *El Norte* are organized around a romantic vision of indigenism, border/*barrio* culture and the return to one's roots. *Born in East L.A.* also tackles these themes, but from a humorous vantage point. The comic technique of director Cheech Marin is similar to what he used in the earlier Cheech and Chong films. There is a broadly played bawdiness about the movie. Yet, *Born in East LA* has many serious overtones in its comedy. The complexity of the thematic development takes this film beyond the level of simple debunking of stereotypes to a new mode of engagement with *Chicanismo* and border discourse.

Marin got the idea for the film while he was reading a newspaper account of a Chicano from East LA who was deported to Mexico. As Marin recounts the story, at the same time he was reading the newspaper, he was listening to Bruce Springsteen's hit, "Born in the USA" on the radio. He wrote and produced a music video parody of the Springsteen rock hit and made the film.

Rosa Linda Fregoso has written about the manner in which *Born in East LA* critiques the reactionary meaning which has come to be associated with the Springsteen version of the song. Fregoso points out that, although the authorial intention of Springsteen was to celebrate working class solidarity and culture, its message was manipulated to meet the xenophobic/patriotic ideology of the Reagan decade. In Fregoso's words: "*Born in the USA* came to signify *US for non-others* (white Anglo-Americans)" and, with that, "foreigners (or non-whites) go home."[52]

Marin's film and video, she says, challenge the predominant construction of American nativeness as white. According to Fregoso, *Born in East L.A.* does this by dismantling the binary system of representation that dominant ideology relies on to enforce racist views of identity and citizenship (i. e. white as native-born and dark as foreign born). She explains how the whites in the film repeatedly refer to non-whites in ethnically ambivalent ways. Fregoso concludes that scenes such as these push the binary system of figuration to its ultimate consequences:

> The film thereby critiques the dominant social discourse of racism which fixes a binary system of representation between native-born and foreign-born in terms of the figurative markers of skin color, or white as native and dark as foreigner. Constructed within the film is a dominant perspective which is unable to differentiate an Asian from an Indian nor a Mexican immigrant from a Chicano native. However, it is an inscription which the film itself dismantles for its viewers. The very cinematic fact that the film allows spectators a knowledge of its

> narrative truth, that Rudy is US-born and that the Asians
> are not Indian, problematizes dominant ideology's racist
> notion of *nativeness*.[53]

Taking Fregoso's argument a bit further, I would contend that Marin's film focuses more other culturally based elements of appearance besides complexion such as socialized forms of expression which provoke racial attitudes and perceptions. This is brought out in a highly complex way in the scenes with the "Asians." For instance, it is interesting to note that two of the actors who play Asians have Hispanic names in the credits. This confounds the problem of defining and representing Hispanic identity, coaxing the audience to consider that many Latin Americans are indeed of Asian descent and that certain Asians (Filipinos) also have Hispanic names. Perhaps Marin's most ironic twist comes at the end of the film in the last scene where the Asians reappear in Los Angeles. As the film concludes, it turns out that because the "Asian" men have learned Chicano mannerisms, they are able to fool the Los Angeles police and escape being apprehended and deported. The Chicano markers of identity imitated by the "Asians" are viewed by the Anglo policeman as native, and guarantee safe passage for Rudy and the other immigrants. The film shows how heavily dependent perceptions of nativeness are based on stereotypes of Chicanos and Mexicans.

There are two ways to approach this problem of reading the stereotyping in *Born in East L.A.* First, is by looking at the range of diversity within the rubric of Mexican coded identity in the film. Second, is to evaluate the comedic style of the film in terms of a Chicano aesthetic called *el rasquachismo*.

There are many other moments in the film where Marin undermines the presumptions of identity. For example, the patterns of Spanish language use by the Mexican and Latin American characters serve as sounding blocks for codes of authenticity implicitly questioned by the discourse of nativeness. This happens in the scene in which the Mexican laborers who are locked in the INS truck with Rudy speak Spanish. Their speech underscores Rudy's alienation from Mexican culture, because he only understands English. The situation also allows Marin to set up a comic scene as the quick witted Rudy becomes the butt of Spanish jokes only the audience (through subtitles) and the Mexican passengers can understand. The Mexican laborers on the bus are depicted in a realistic mode of presentation in the scene. Their clever sarcasm and sense of superiority towards Rudy, who they regard as *pocho* (a denigrating term for an Americanized Mexican), inscribes them with a humanity and dignity that challenges the traditional portrayal of the migrant as victim or opportunist and in this instance, allows the audience to identify with Spanish as the language of the dominant culture.

Unlike the Cheech and Chong films which maintain a consistently absurd tone, in *Born in East L.A.* Cheech Marin maneuvers between modes of reality arbitrarily shifting between realism and parody. This is also the technique which is most likely to have motivated one white reviewer to characterize *Born in East L.A.* as nothing more than "a string of uneven skits."[54] Chon Noriega has pointed out that Anglo film critics often write negative reviews of Chicano features, criticizing them for unevenness, confusing style or rambling characterizations. Noriega maintains these comments are evidence of the critics' refusal to acknowledge ethnically inspired cinematic forms.[55] Following from this, I would like to discuss Marin's cinematic technique (what white reviewers characterize as "erratic" style) in terms of his use of *rasquachismo*.

Tomás Ybarra-Frausto describes *rasquachismo* as a Chicano sensibility: much like an a attitude or a taste. He develops the following definition:

> 1. Very generally, *rasquachismo* is an underdog perspective, a view from *los de abajo*, an attitude rooted in resourcefulness and adaptability yet mindful of stance and style.

> 2. *Rasquachismo* presupposes the world view of the have-not, but is also a quality exemplified in objects and places (a *rasquache* car or restaurant), and in social comportment (a person can be or act *rasquache*).

> 3. Mexican vernacular traditions form the base of *rasquachismo*, but it has evolved as a bicultural sensibility among Mexican Americans. On both sides of the border, it retains an underclass perspective.[56]

He adds that *rasquachismo* is associated with vulgarity and bad taste and notes that, only recently, has it been adopted by the university educated generation of Chicano artists. To have a *rasquache* attitude is to be able to creatively make due with the little that you have: "*Rasquachismo* is a compendium of all the *movidas* (coping strategies) displayed in immediate day to day living."[57]

The *rasquache* tradition can be traced back to the 1930's and 1940's when traveling vaudeville acts (*tandas de variedad*) and tent shows (*carpa*) played the Southwest, presenting robust slapstick theatrical sketches. The carpa skits had as staple characters the *peladito* and *peladita*, impoverished urban survivors who embodied the archetypal Chicano every man and every woman. In the other Chicano art forms, *rasquachismo* is typified by bold display, ornamentation and a preference for shimmering colors."[58]

As Marin transgresses the borders between fantasy and reality he captures the border *rasquache* sensibility. Take, for instance, the visual contrast between the INS processing site, where meticulous attention has been paid to simulating the fluorescent lighting and filling the scene with dozens of extras, and the surreal electrocution chamber set. The highly stylized room in the jail is designed like a tattoo parlor with hundreds of Chicano/Mexican images painted on the walls. Marin gives us no transitions or narrative explanation for the sudden appearance of the surreal episode. He prefers to cut randomly between reality and hyperbole. I would argue that the jolt we feel at style switching creates the border *sabor* (flavor) of the film and is part of Marin's own *rascuache* aesthetic, not a flaw in form.

Ybarra-Frausto provides a "random list" of *rasquachismo* where he includes *Born in East L.A.* under the "low *rasquachismo*" category along with the early *actos* of El Teatro Campesino and paintings on velvet.[59] From the vantage point of the *rasquache* aesthetic, one can read Marin's shift between a realist and a parodic stance, not as a clumsy approach at Aristotelian structure, but as a *movida* (coping strategy). His blending of styles can be seen as a more fruitful tactic for dealing with point of view and the multicultural identities of the border characters which are so crucial in the film. For the *rasquache* artist, reality and identity can only be understood as a dialogic process, constantly redefining, continually in flux.

CONCLUSION

Chicano features offer a highly complex and varied articulation of the border experience. Drawing upon certain established Chicano artistic practices such as *el rasquachismo* and the *barrio* aesthetic, the four films in this chapter develop a discourse on border culture that at times approaches a radical critique of ethnocentrism and cultural imperialism. All four movies look to the other side of the border and beyond, ultimately creating a Pan-Latin American framework for Chicano cultural politics. As a group, these films ask us to bypass a simplistic definition of Chicano identity as a collective "one true self." Instead, we must conclude that the identity expressed through these cinematic artifacts is one of process, a perpetual state of self-conscious actualization, of "*mestización*," and a positioning of identity within the range of Pan-Latin American multicultural influences.

NOTES

1. Migration of Anglos into the newly conquered territory coincided with the gold rush of 1848. Within one year 80,000 Anglos had entered the California territory and by 1852 the population of the region swelled to a quarter million. Between 1850 and 1924 there was a continual movement of people back and forth between Mexico and the United States until the Border Patrol was established in 1924. See, Julian Samora, "Mexican Immigration," in *Introduction to Chicano Studies*, ed. Livie Isauro Duran and H. Russell Bernard (New York: MacMillan, 1973), pp. 230 -246.

2. For an overview of the cultural exchange which took place between these diverse ethnic influences see Shifra Goldman and Tomás Ybarra-Frausto, *Arte Chicano* (Berkeley: University of California, Chicano Studies Library Publications Unit, 1985).

3. For an overview of Chicano/Border Art see special issue of *Imagine: International Journal of Chicano Poetry* (Winter, 1991).

4. See exhibition catalogues and program notes by David Avalos and Philip Brookman, *Café Mestizo (David Avalos)* (New York: INTAR, 1989).

5. Border music has had a long history in the region. For an overview of the history of Tex Mex music see Onofre Antonio Abarca, "Viva la Onda Chicana: A Personal Perspective on Tex-Mex Music," in *Forward: A Journal of Socialist Thought* 8 (Spring 1988): 83-93. A second important form of border music, known as the *corrido*, has its roots in the Spanish *romance* and

continues to be performed by local musicians in the Southwest. See Américo Paredes, *With His Pistol in Hand: A Border Ballad and Its Hero* (Austin: University of Texas Press, 1971).

6. Emily Hicks, "What the Broken Line is Not," *La Linea Quebrada/The Broken Line Troupe No. 2* (San Diego: Centro Cultural de La Raza, 1985).

7. Guillermo Gómez-Peña, "Border Culture and Deterritorialization," in *La Linea Quebrada Troupe No. 2* (San Diego: Centro Cultural de La Raza, 1985).

8. Guillermo Gómez-Peña, "Death on the Border: A Eulogy to Border Art," *High Performance* 14 (Spring, 1991): 8.

9. Ibid., p. 9.

10. I refer to these films as a social justice genre, wherein the protagonist becomes the focal point of systematic social injustice. *Sandino* (1990), *Mpantsula* (1987), *Under Fire* (1983) *The Killing Fields* (1984) would be encompassed in the genre. Many of these films also fall within what Claudia Springer has identified as the Third World investigation film genre which typically positions the spectator in the role of cultural outsider identifying with the reporter/protagonist who acts as interpreter of the foreign experience. Claudia Springer, "Comprehension and Crisis: Reporter Films and the Third World," in *Unspeakable Images: Ethnicity and the American Cinema* ed. Lester Friedman (Urbana: University of Illinois Press, 1990), pp. 167-190.

11. Jorge Ayala Blanco, "Artenstein y el Mito del Cine Chicano," *El Financiero*, 10 Sept. 1990, Cultural Sec., p. 71.

12. Gloria Anzaldúa, *Borderlands/La Frontera: The New Mestiza* (San Francisco: Spinsters/Aunt Lute Book Co., 1987), p. 54.

13. *Ibid.*, p. 53.

14. Tomás Ybarra-Frausto, "Tomás Ybarra-Frausto on Mestizaje," *Cine de Mestizaje* (NY: El Museo del Barrio, 1991), p. 26.

15. The Treaty of Guadalupe-Hidalgo contained democratic guarantees which could have allowed for an integration of Chicano culture into the larger society. It contained provisions to protect the land, language, religious and political rights of the conquered Mexicans living in the Southwest. These provisions were never honored.

16. Felix Padilla, *Latino Ethnic Consciousness: The Case of Mexican Americans and Puerto Ricans in Chicago* (Notre Dame: University of Notre Dame Press, 1985), pp. 61-79.

17. For further discussion of the use of Spanish as a competing alternative public discourse see, Flores and Yúdice, "Living Borders/Buscando America: Languages of Latino Self-formation," *Social Text: Theory/Culture/Ideology* 8.2 (1990): 57-84.

18. The main organization behind the English-only Movement is "U.S. English." Claiming more than 300,000 dues paying members, the predominantly White organization hired a Chicana, Linda Chavez (former

Reagan appointee to the U.S. Civil Rights Commission), as its national spokesperson. The group has been successful in obtaining the passage of English-only laws in California and Florida, states with high Latino/a populations. According to Teresa Montano and Dennis Vigil the fundamental reason for the attack on Spanish speaking Americans is because Latinos pose a strategic threat to monopoly capitalist control of the southwestern United States. They argue that the Latino population explosion in the sunbelt region will destabilize the area, leading to massive Chicano uprisings in the next century. This threat is understood by the White bourgeoisie, and, hence, the upsurge in efforts to acculturate Chicanos by decimating their language. See "English-only: Right Wing's Power of Babble," in *Forward: A Journal of Socialist Thought* 8 (Spring, 1988): 51-83.

19. The Simpson-Rodino law mandated strong penalties against employers of "illegal" immigrants. The bill has been criticized by Chicano groups who say that it unfairly targets Mexican immigrants and promotes anti-Latino sentiment throughout the country.

20. Since 1929, U.S. policy towards Mexican immigration has vacillated considerably. During periods of economic prosperity when labor shortages occurred in the Southwest, Mexicans have been encouraged to cross the border. When the economic climate shifts, Mexican immigrants have been and continue to be expelled in large numbers. For an historical account of this immigration history see Juan Ramón García, *Operation Wetback: The Mass Deportation of Mexican Undocumented Workers in 1954* (Westport, CT: Greenwood Press, 1980); and Abraham Hoffman, *Unwanted Mexican-Americans in the Great Depression* (Tucson: University of Arizona Press, 1974).

21. The Mexican Revolution was a major factor in the displacement of Mexicans to the U.S. Many soldiers and supporters of revolutionary leaders like Villa, Obregón, Carranza and Zapata fled political persecution from their own government. Although a publication of the National Bureau of Economic Research puts the number close to two hundred thousand, it is probable that close to one million Mexicans crossed over into the United States between 1910 and 1920. See Meier and Rivera, *The Chicanos: A History of Mexican Americans* (New York: Hill and Wang, 1972), p. 235.

22. For instance, the Magón brothers published *Regeneración* in San Antonio, St. Louis and El Pasa. Later, while in Los Angeles, Ricardo Flores Magón published *La Revolución*. In southeastern Arizona, Praxedis Guerero organized copper miners into a union called Obreros Libres (Free Workers). See Meier and Rivera, *The Chicanos*, p. 119-123.

23. Armando Navarro, "The Evolution of Chicano Politics," *Aztlán: A Journal of Chicano Studies* 5 (Fall 1972): 61.

24. The Mexican Constitution of 1917 gave the Mexican nation exclusive rights to subsoil minerals.

25. Kenneth F. Johnson, *Mexican Democracy: A Critical View* (New York: Praeger, 1978), p. 44.

26. For an explanation of how these references play a part in Chicano Art see *Chicano Art: Resistance and Affirmation* (Los Angeles: UCLA Wight Art Gallery, 1990).

27. Anzaldúa, *Borderlands*, p. 54.

28. For further discussion of Spanish language radio stations in the U.S. see Felix Gutiérrez and Jorge Reina Schemendt, *Spanish Language Radio in the United States* (Austin: University of Texas Press, 1979).

29. Teshome Gabriel, "Thesis on Memory and Identity: In Search of the Origin of the River Nile," *Emergences* 1: 130-137.

30. Chon Noriega, "Ensayo: Above all Raza must speak: we have much to say and it must be heard," (New York: Museo del Barrio, 1991).

31. Rosa Linda Fregoso notes that the scene depicts and actual incident which occurred in southern Texas. Rosa Linda Fregoso, *The Bronze Screen: Chicana and Chicano Film Culture* (Minneapolis: University of Minnesota Press, 1993), p. 85.

32. Salazar was killed when he was struck by a tear gas canister that was fired into a crowd by police. For an historical account of violence against the Chicano Movement consult Carlos Muñoz Jr., *Youth, Identity, Power*.

33. Ibid,, p. 52.

34. Ana López, "An Other History: The New Latin American Cinema," *Radical History Review* 42, (Spring 1988): 93-116.

35. José Angel Guitiérrez, "The Chicano in Mexicano-Norte Americano Foreign Relations," in *Chicano-Mexicano Relations*, eds. Tatcho Mindiola Jr. and Max Martinez (University Park: University of Houston Press, 1986), p. 28.

36. Camplís, "Towards the Development of a Raza Cinema," p. 5.

37. Carlos Monsivaís, "The Culture of the Frontier: The Mexican Side," in *Views from Across the Border*, ed. Stanley Ross (Albuquerque: University of New Mexico, 1978), p. 54.

38. Ibid., p. 55.

39. In Guatemala, when someone is kidnapped by the army, they are often tortured and their body is hidden. The practice is referred to as "disappearing." Since 1954, when the C.I.A. orchestrated the overthrown of the democratically elected government of Guatemalan President Arbenz, more than 100,000 people have been disappeared in Guatemala.

40. Dolores Prida, "*El Norte*: A Landmark Latino Film," *Nuestro* (May, 1984), p. 49.

41. Alejo Carpentier, *El siglo de las luces* (Caracas: Biblioteca Ayacucho, 1979).

42. Ibid., p. xi.

43. Mayan women weave their communal history into their native dress. Each color and pattern represents a different aspect of Mayan cosmology.

44. Lucila Vargas, "EL Norte," in *The Americas Review* 14 (Spring 1986): 25.

45. For a general analysis of the economic and political situation in Guatemala consult, Jonathan Fried, ed., *Guatemala in Rebellion* (New York: Grove Press, 1983) and *Guatemala: Eternal Spring, Eternal Tyranny* (New York: W.W. Norton and Company, 1987).

46. Herbert Marcuse, *A Critique of Pure Tolerance* (Boston: Beacon Press, 1969), pp. 84-85.

47. David Rosen, *Off Hollywood: The Making and Marketing of Independent Films* (New York: Grove Weidenfeld, 1990), pp. 59-77.

48. For an account of the role of the indigenous population in armed resistance movements in Guatemala consult Rigoberta Menchu, *I Rigoberta Menchu: An Indian Woman in Guatemala* (London: Verso, 1984).

49. Rosen, *Off Hollywood*, p. 66.

50. Ibid., p. 67.

51. In March of 1987 *El Norte* was shown on PBS in Chicago. It was introduced as a film about Guatemalans who decide to immigrate to the U.S. because of land disputes. This reductionistic explanation of the film angered Guatemalan refugee groups in the city who responded with phone calls of protest against the station.

52. Rosa Linda Fregoso, "*Born in East L.A.* and the Politics of Representation," *Cultural Studies*, No. 4 (October 1990): 271. For a slightly different treatment of the film by Fregoso see *The Bronze Screen*, pp. 49-64.

53. Ibid., p. 273.

54. Tom Cunniff, *People Weekly*, 14 September 1987, p. 14.

55. Noriega, *Road to Aztlán*, pp. 216-257.

56. Tomás Ybarra-Frausto, "*Rasquachismo;* A Chicano sensibility in Chicano Aesthetics," (Phoenix: MARS Inc. Exhibition Catalog, 1987), p. 5.

57. Ibid.

58. Ibid., p. 6.

59. Ibid., p. 7.

V

GENDER AND GENRE
IN *ONLY ONCE IN A LIFETIME*

From 1935 until the late seventies only ten films dealing with Chicano protagonists and subject matter were produced in the United States.[1] Two of those films, *Boulevard Nights* (1979) and *Walk Proud* (1979) were gang style exploitation films. The others can be categorized as Mexican social-problem films, a genre which raises issues of ethnicity in an overt manner as part of the main plot rather than as subtext.[2] Movies in this genre work through social conflicts in a way which diffuses contradiction. Racial problems posed in the narrative are consistently resolved with "safe" solutions and reinforce prevailing Anglo perspectives on the place of Chicanos in U.S. society. Protagonists in social problem films are shown resigning themselves to segregation in the *barrio* or assimilating into the mainstream Anglo culture.[3] The narrative structure of many of the older social problem films centers around the story of a Mexican American male who is excessively violent or socially misfit. This outcast character must learn to accept his place in the white society. This resolution is achieved most often through the patronizing guidance of an Anglo authority figure, or, in the case of *A Medal for Benny*, *The Ring*, and *Right Cross*, the "civilizing" force is provided by a female lover who harnesses the anti-white impulses of the Mexican American male protagonist through her domesticating influences.

Chon Noriega has analyzed the narrative structure of these Hollywood films. He unveils the complex ideological function of their stories in the context of the xenophobic American political climate of the time. The decades in which these films were produced marked an era in which the U.S. government carried out a number of anti-Mexican programs. The effect of these programs was to terrorize the

Mexican American population and to heighten anti-Mexican American sentiment among Anglos.

For a generation prior to this (during World War I and on in to the twenties) a new wave of immigrants had come to the U.S. from Mexico with relatively little threat of deportation. But the massive unemployment of the depression led the U.S. government to initiate a repatriation program which resulted in the deportation of some 400,000 Mexicans, Mexican Americans and others legally residing in this country. The Mexican American middle class attempted to fight the growing tide of racism by forming a network of social service organizations designed to present a united front and promote assimilation. But their success was minimal. Big business set U.S. immigration policy according to their fluctuating need for cheap agricultural labor in the Southwest.

Similar schizophrenic procedures were carried out in the forties and fifties. Under the "Bracero" Program, Mexican laborers were encouraged to enter this country only to be deported once again as the government arrested some 2.9 million "illegal aliens" under the authority of "Operation Wetback." As before, the deportation program had the effect of suppressing the civil rights of Mexican Americans. Workers who attempted to organize were forced to give up their jobs. Through manipulation of deportation laws a significant number of political and labor activists were exiled.[4]

It was within this context of government sanctioned repression that Hollywood generated its version of the Mexican American "problem." As with most other ethnic problem films put out by Hollywood, socio-economic factors were not addressed. Racial and ethnic questions were diffused and absorbed into broader U.S. national problems such as juvenile delinquency or gender relations. In this way, the central problem of equal rights and citizenship, which was at the heart of the Mexican American social movement of the time, could be conveniently avoided.

In *Only Once in a Lifetime* (written and directed by Alejandro Grattan and produced by Moctesuma Esparza, 1978) the traditional genre elements characteristic of the Mexican American social problem film have been reworked from a Chicano perspective. The plot of the film is initiated with a scene in which a county agricultural inspector orders the protagonist, Francisco Domínguez, an aging Chicano widower, to stop growing vegetables on his small plot of land in East

Los Angeles. This garden has been Francisco's only means of support. Losing the garden, coupled with the fact that he is unable to earn a living from his true talent, oil painting, sends Francisco into deep depression. He is further demoralized when an Anglo social worker tries to force him to file for public aid. This pushes Francisco to contemplate taking his own life.

The scenes of Francisco's interaction with the welfare state constitute a significant reversal of the Hollywood portrayal of the role of white institutions in the Chicano community. In the older films, intermediaries such as educators, coaches, lawyers and judges are shown as sympathetic facilitators encouraging the peaceful assimilation of marginalized Mexican Americans into Anglo society. In contrast to the Hollywood approach, the opening sequences in *Only Once in a Lifetime* posit white intervention in the *barrio* as a causal factor of the ineffectual and nihilistic outlook of the Chicano protagonist. The theme of nihilism is further developed when the director complicates the initial plot line, shifting focus on Francisco's situation as a Chicano artist. The film posits that Francisco is unable to survive in a white controlled economy unless he gives up his tragic vision of the *barrio* and paints more positive depictions of Chicano life. But he can see nothing positive to paint, only a bleak reality. For Francisco, the world is dark and sad. When his pieces are occasionally displayed in a friend's gallery, the patrons (wealthy Anglos) show disinterest with this type of art. The gallery owner encourages him to compromise his artistic vision, one which is deeply rooted in his own experiences in the *barrio*.

As the social problem discourse continues to unfold a major deviation in the story line occurs. Francisco's narrative becomes a secondary plot as the film shifts focus and a new plot is introduced. This competing plot is structured in the form of a melodrama. The love interest is Consuelo, a thirty five year old Chicana school teacher who Francisco meets when her father agrees to take care of Francisco's dog. Puzzled over why Francisco would give away his dog, Consuelo suspects something is wrong, and after a series of casual meetings, Francisco and Consuelo begin to fall in love with each other. In the end, her kindness lifts him out of his depression and inspires him to paint a portrait that is beautiful and uplifting, a work of art which the narrative indicates will surely be purchased. But Consuelo is a woman who is at a crossroads in her life. Her father, an entrepreneur fed up with the problems of the *barrio*, is about to move her to the West side (the Anglo side) of the city. Unless she can find a "suitable" husband to take care of her, Consuelo's father will insist that she go along. Her impending decision becomes the competing social problem in the film. She must choose whether or not to disobey her father's will and stay in the *barrio*.

In the final scene of the film, Consuelo does decide not to move and to remain on the east side and teach in a Chicana elementary school. Her decision to stay can be differentiated from similar plot resolutions found in the older Hollywood social problem films. Consuelo's choice is not premised on a psycho/social maladjustment in her character as she would relate to a broader Anglo world. In the earlier Hollywood social problem films, the Mexican American chooses the *barrio* only after he learns the lesson that he was wrong to think that the Anglo society was/is the cause of his oppression. In *Only Once in a Lifetime*, Consuelo's decision represents a new horizon of narrative options, choices which are Chicano specific. She is not opting in this film between either joining the Anglo world or her Chicano one. Participating in Anglo society has never been her ambition. Instead, Consuelo is facing a choice between either maintaining the traditional family structure and its prescribed gender roles or disobeying her father and thereby asserting a new feminine independence. The second social problem centered around the love story plot is not, therefore, one addressed to the expectations of white viewers, encouraging them to understand the Mexican American's "deserved" separatism or need to assimilate. In this film, the problem is spoken to a specifically Chicano audience, though it certainly could speak to all women who feel imprisoned by traditional patriarchal family structures.

LA CHICANA AND *LA FAMILIA*

Research completed by Chicana scholars on the topic of la Chicana and her place in the Chicana family confirms a view of *la familia* as, generally, a constraining social formation for women. Sociologist Betty García Bahne has explained how family values like "loyalty" are the cornerstone of male domination, maintaining woman's dependency. She also writes about the political implication of other traditional "feminine" values that are reinforced within the Chicana family unit such as modesty and reserved behavior of women. She concludes that these social values keep women from learning skills that could lead them to economic independence. She goes on to argue that many women who uphold such values often come to believe that they must be cared for and be passive.[5]

During the social movements of the sixties and seventies the traditional role of women in *la familia* was at first reinforced. Chicano nationalism became synonymous with home and *la familia Chicana*:

> What are the common denominators that unite the people?
> The key common denominator is nationalism . . .
> nationalism becomes La familia. Nationalism comes first
> out of the family, then into tribalism and then into alliances
> that are necessary to lift the burden of all suppressed
> humanity.[6]

Many in the Movement recognized that *la familia* had operated as a mechanism of cultural resistance by affording protection, comfort, security and a space for a Chicano identity in a system characterized by destroying cultural distinctions. Yet it soon became apparent to the politicized women in the Movement that this romantic notion of *la familia* glossed over questions of egalitarianism which were surfacing among those who felt marginalized within male controlled Movement organizations. Chicana historian, Sonia López, says that as early as 1970 Chicana students were issuing feminist manifestos challenging the patriarchal treatment Chicanas had received by comrades. In some cases alternative Chicana organizations were formed:[7]

> As soon as I started expounding my own ideas the men
> who ran the organization would either ignore my statement,
> or make a wisecrack about it and continue their own
> discussion. This continued for two years until I finally
> broke away because of being unable to handle the
> situation.[8]

The challenges to traditional gender roles continued to grow causing some Chicanos to question their own views on relations within the family.[9] *Only Once in a Lifetime* was produced within this era of reevaluation of traditional configurations of *la familia* and of the contradictions embedded within traditional patriarchal culture. Yet upon further examination of the narrative structure of the film, one sees that the movie does not go far enough in questioning gender relations. Instead the film's problematic ending tends to replicate androcentric constructions of identity. When the character Consuelo chooses to be with Francisco, the relationship between father and daughter is not transformed or questioned. The director merely uses the conventions of the love story genre to reproduce the structure of psychological dependency that controls Consuelo's actions, thereby circumscribing her agency within the traditional parameters of *la familia*. By casting her decision within the framework of a love story, the narrative possibilities are necessarily restricted. The melodrama ends up directing the audience's desire towards fulfillment of Consuelo as a female subject through marriage and away from the social problem of assimilation initially proposed by the text.

ROMANTIC MELODRAMA
AND ASSIMILATION DISCOURSE

Melodrama is a style of storytelling which is often explained in its relationship to realism. However, since the interpretation of realism has shifted over the decades in accordance with artistic trends and new critical perspectives, the notion of melodrama as employing excessive as opposed to "realistic" acting, music or emotion becomes very problematic. Melodrama is also an expansive category which spans various genres. Often these genres are aimed at specifically gendered audiences.[10] Many genres of melodrama are targeted predominantly toward women, and, because of this, melodrama has become an active site for feminist cultural studies. These studies conclude that melodramas aimed at women elicit both progressive and regressive attitudes in their viewers.[11]

In Latin America, melodrama is marketed to women in the form of popular paperback *photonovelas* and via television soap operas called *telenovelas*. The most popular form of narrative television entertainment in Latin America, *telenovelas* dominate Spanish language television. The form resembles English language soap opera but the number of shows is limited (with the series lasting between two to four hundred episodes). Episodes are aired at all times of the day and are watched by women and sometimes men. The *telenovelas* are produced in several different countries including Venezuela, Cuba, Brazil,

Argentina, Mexico and Puerto Rico and occupy the best prime time slots.[12]

Ana López points out that this tremendously successful aesthetic form was at first rejected by the radical filmmakers of the New Latin American Cinema Movement (NLACM). Lopez sights the Movement's original commitment to battling imperialist art and media as a cause of their antagonism towards the form. The NLACM associated melodrama with mass culture and determined that it falsely directed viewers' desires away from issues of national importance. In its place, progressive Latin American directors tried to make didactic films which would recover their national history. Eventually, several filmmakers came back to the genre and tried to deconstruct and foreground narrative conventions of the form. For instance, in *Lucía* (1968) Humberto Solas successfully deployed a critique of various kinds of melodramatic styles by constructing an episodic narrative. Another Cuban film *Cecilia* (1983) used Marxist techniques of class analysis to adapt a well known melodramatic novel by Cerilo Villaverde (*Cecilia Valdés*) for the screen. The directors of the NLACM were eventually able to embrace melodramatic forms in politically challenging ways because they wanted to meet the real needs and desires of audiences. The melodramas of the NLACM approximated the kind of "popular" culture that Latin American theorists and filmmakers had been espousing since the 1960s; a cinema which politicizes the culture of the masses.

The Chicano filmmaking community never seemed to get caught up in the same ideological argument against melodrama that characterized the early years of the NLACM. One of the first television programs created by Chicanos was a *telenovela* called *Canción de la raza* (1968-1970).[13] Similarly, one of the first Chicano features was a low budget melodrama *Amor chicano es para siempre* (by directors Efraín Gutiérrez and Josie Faz, 1977). Today, the *telenovela* is being used throughout the Latino community to make Spanish tapes about AIDS.[14]

In choosing to work with melodrama, the director and producer of *Only Once in a Life Time*, aligned Chicano Cinema with the *telenovela* tradition and underscored a commitment to film as an entertainment vehicle. But the Chicano Cinema Movement has also characterized itself as a progressive cinema. As such, it is important when looking at Chicano melodrama to keep in mind the criticisms voiced by the founding members of the NLACM. They remind us that while the melodrama is a popular form of entertainment, it still can be used as a vehicle of ideological conservatism. A critical view of the way certain conventions of the melodrama function makes it possible for filmmakers to rework elements of the form that might otherwise colonize viewers.

Only Once in a Life Time is both a social problem film and a love story. The social problem discourse,(whether or not to stay in the *barrio*) is, however, not the focus of the protagonist's story. Francisco, the main character, is oppressed by racism but is also shown to suffer from a personal crisis attributed to an individual problem. His depression is, in great part, associated with the death of his first wife and the need to express himself as an individual, not only as a Chicano artist. The narrative dilemma raised through his character is to choose between continuing to paint fatalistic images of the Chicano working class (thus, facing possible starvation) and betraying his own idiosyncratic vision by making art which can be sold for profit. The standard social problem plot line which deals with taking responsibility for the *barrio* is not worked out via Francisco, but, rather, is laid on Consuelo's shoulders. She is the one saddled with the momentous burden of deciding whether or not to stay with her people. Though she chooses to stay, the potential strength of her decision is undercut by the fact that the film leads the viewer to believe that it is Consuelo's love for Francisco which ultimately motivates her actions. In the final analysis, it is the conventional framework of the romance genre that structures the social problem discourse and circumscribes the agency of the female character, diminishing what would have been a heroic act under other circumstances.

Mary Ann Doane has outlined parameters and devices of the Hollywood love story in her book, *The Desire to Desire: The Woman's Film of the 1940's.*[15] She notes that the love story is typically regarded as a format which speaks to women spectators and therefore has been ghettoized in the codification of film history. The ordinary love story is perceived as "opportunistic" in its manipulation of affect; over-relying on music and emotion. She also agrees with Roland Barthes' assessment of the genre that the male character in a romance story is somewhat feminized after being "contaminated" by the elements of the genre. She points to the existence of the subgenre, the artist as lover story, as a way Hollywood has devised to integrate the male character into the feminine realm of feelings and emotions. Art in this subgenre becomes the male protagonist's culturally sanctioned "feminized activity," serving as a legitimate avenue for male sensitivity to be expressed.

This melodramatic structure is also used in *Only Once in a Life Time*. Francisco, a painter, is a man who sincerely cares about women. He is shown at the grave of his beautiful young wife, confiding his deepest emotions. In a flashback, he is resting with his head in her lap, granting her a more dominant posture in the frame. In another scene, Francisco is approached by a woman in a movie theater. She is an out of work alcoholic actress who invites him to her room, presumably for a sexual encounter. Instead of pursuing intercourse with her, he offers her a glass of milk and gently tucks her into bed, providing her with much needed compassion. Francisco's passivity in these scenes, momentarily, provides the female viewer with an appealing, alternative, feminized object of desire. But unfortunately, the film undermines its own feminized point of view by making Francisco's passivity (portrayed to the point of emasculation) into a pivotal conflict which must be resolved in the narrative. The text argues that the "feminine side" of his personality has become too dominant and has taken over his life and his art. Francisco overempathizes with the misery of his surroundings, limiting his ability to act effectively in his personal life and in his art. Through his increasing desire for Consuelo, however, Francisco regains his self esteem and attains a renewed ability to resist the demoralizing attitudes of the Anglo welfare workers who have also tried to emasculate him through their patronizing intrusion into his life. Thus, it is the increasing momentum of the love story which restores the male protagonist to an active position in the text by interposing an even more passive female character into the story line.

In her analysis of female characters in the love stories of the 1940s, Mary Ann Doane asserts that the woman protagonist, in her passive position, must always give up something for the sake of her love.[16] Abiding by this convention is exactly what devalues the political content of the female character's decision to remain in the *barrio* in *Only Once in a Lifetime*. When Consuelo goes against her father and stays on the East Side, it is presented as an expression of her love for Francisco rather than as a political act of commitment to her people. In earlier scenes, she does appear upset about moving out of the *barrio* but only acts upon her feelings after Francisco shows romantic interest in her.

This privileging of the love story plot over the plot about commitment to *La Raza* is especially evident when one considers that there are no scenes which show Consuelo working in the community. She says she is a teacher in East Los Angeles who loves her students, but the film never actually gives the audience any scenes with Consuelo becoming actively involved in anything. Her principal narrative action is to nurture Francisco.

CHICANAS REWRITE
THE CULTURAL LEGACY OF ROMANCE

The aura of "romantic love" has been used throughout history to explain women's actions and, in the process, devalue them. Chicana scholars have exposed this sexist practice of storytelling as it is manifested in Mexican and Mexican American culture. Norma Cantú, for example, grapples with what she terms, the "Adelita complex." Adelitas (or *soldaderas* from the Mexican Revolution) have come to connote followers, or a woman following a man into battle out of love and commitment to *him*. Cantú says such interpretation of the *soldaderas* obscures the fact that these women were not merely followers but also military strategists and warriors themselves.[17]

Adelaída Del Castillo exposes the contradictions of "La Malinche," a Mexican legend that subsumes a woman's political action in the tale of a misguided love affair.[18] The story is that of Marina, La Malinche, a legend passed down through Mexican and Mexican American culture since the time of the Spanish Invasion. According to the legend, an Aztec princess, Malintzín Tenepal, fell in love with Hernán Cortez while serving as his translator. Her deep love for him eventually led her to become his accomplice in the destruction of the Aztec empire. She also bore him a child who became known as the first person of mixed or *mestizo* heritage in Latin America. La Malinche is regarded as the first person to betray the indigenous collectivity. She is the Eve of Mexican culture, a woman who contaminated the purity of the native race with European blood. She is regarded as the person responsible for the fall of the continent, and is referred to as *la vendida* (the sellout). She is also known as *la chingada*, the one who was violated by Cortez, and it is a common belief (like in the Adam and Eve tale of European culture) that her action generated evil in all those of the female sex. The notion of La Malinche as the "*chingada*" is also used to justify the view of women as naturally passive and, following the same logic, a view of men as active agents and penetrators. Del Castillo offers a particularly offensive quote from the Mexican philosopher Octavio Paz to underscore the ridiculous degree to which Paz and others have used the Malinche legend to reinforce their views on female passivity:

> The Chingada [La Malinche] is even more passive. Her passivity is abject: she does not resist violence, but is an inert heap of bones, blood and dust.[19]

Del Castillo disagrees with the patriarchal interpretation of Doña Marina and proposes an alternative history of Marina's actions. She points out that the Aztec elites were brutal despots engaging in a reign of terror over other tribes in the region. Doña Marina was, in reality, a compassionate diplomat who consciously tried to avoid a series of massacres carried out by male rulers from all sides. Her abilities as translator between the cultures prevented annihilation of the indigenous population and helped preserve sacred elements of the culture.

From the vantage point of these feminist rewritings, one can deconstruct the ideological traps that a popular genre like the romantic melodrama set for the male director of *Only Once in a Life Time*. While the film successfully undermined the social problem genre by diffusing the conventional discourse on separatism and assimilation, it could not help but become entangled by the patriarchal conventions of the love story which go unchallenged. According to Modleski, in a love story the "feminized" man is attractive "because of the freedom he seems to offer the woman: freedom to get in touch with and to act upon her own desire and freedom to reject patriarchal power."[20] This freedom is, however, in the end, illusory because the woman's only significant action, sacrificing something to be with her lover is, in itself, an act of denial which, ironically, only further confirms her passivity through the action. In *Only Once in a Lifetime*, Consuelo's rejection of a life with her domineering father for a life with Francisco recasts Consuelo's action (staying in the *barrio* and leaving her father) into a passive reaction. She is not going from the position of daughter to woman, but from the position of daughter to wife.

HEARTBREAKER

Written by Vincente Gutiérrez and directed by Frank Zuniga, former President of the Hispanic Media Coalition, *Heartbreaker* (1983) is the story of romance. It is the love story between a young Chicano named Beto who is the president of a car club and an Anglo shampoo girl who has the "badest blue eyes" in town. *Heartbreaker* has the blond, Kim, move out of her Anglo environment into the *barrio*. Though there is one very brief scene in the beginning where she tells the handsome Beto that things can't work out between them, cross cultural love is not the focus of the plot as it would be in a social problem film.[21] Rather, the obstacle the two lovers face in achieving a perfect union is Hector, Beto's longtime rival. Hector is a corrupt Chicano who is out to compromise the integrity of the local car clubs by unfairly influencing the results of an upcoming competition. He was also dating Kim before she fell for Beto and suffers from jealousy. To reestablish his control, Hector breaks into Kim's apartment one night and tries to rape her. Kim refuses to see any men after that, but, finally succumbs to Beto's tender pleas and makes love to him. The sex scene becomes a symbolic marriage between the young couple. The last twenty minutes of the film are devoted to Beto fighting bad guys and bringing Hector to justice.

With *Heartbreaker* the filmmaker was apparently attempting to appeal to the car club culture so popular in Los Angeles at the time. But unfortunately, the film degenerates into a sexist romantic fantasy. The film opens with Kim waiting in a hair salon to fall for the right guy. At first she doesn't realize Beto is the right one for her, but eventually comes to her senses. Like in *Only Once in a Lifetime*, Kim decides to move out of her parents house, asserting her own independence from her domineering (and bigoted) father. Also, as in *Only Once in a Lifetime*, breaking away from the family is only a rite of passage for Kim from one patriarchal relationship to another. As soon as Kim has sex with Beto, she becomes his and her place in the narrative becomes extremely passive, almost nonexistent. In fact, she has no active part in the story after that point. Her function within the frame converts to pure decoration. Dressed in "sexy" clothing, she hangs on to Beto and serves as a display model for his car. Zuniga is obviously trying to imitate car club culture in which it is prestigious for young Chicano men to drape their cars with beautiful women (see *Low*

Rider Magazine for examples). This image of Kim posing on Beto's car while he photographs her, reduces her place in the narrative to the literal status of a classic collectible (She is his white trophy).[22] In effect, Kim's identity, although passive, is erased by having the climax to the love plot come much too soon in the film. Leaving the couple devoted to each other for the last twenty minutes in the story, opened up enough narrative time for the director to annihilate the woman altogether.

CHICANA VOICES

At the same time Chicanos were working on their features, Chicanas were developing their own oppositional cinematic aesthetic. Rosa Linda Fregoso explains how women filmmakers chose to look for alternatives after being marginalized by Movement artists whose notions of political art often served to justify androcentrism and to discredit films and tapes made by women.[23] The men could not depict Chicanas as historical agents of political or aesthetic struggle. Their marginalization of Chicana filmmakers was structured into the very institutions that established the canons of Chicano cinema (film festivals and scholarly work on the history of Chicano Cinema).[24] Fregoso maintains that one of the reasons why Chicanas were so excluded was that they worked in shorter formats than the men. Their "smaller" films were not recognized because of the way phallocentric society privileges bigness, power and "penetration into the Hollywood market." In response to marginalization and also as a general outgrowth of their search for appropriate forms to express their experiences, Chicana filmmakers have established a body of short narratives, experimental films and documentaries which pose an aesthetic counterpoint to the Chicano feature.[25]

Replies of the Night, by Sandra Hahn, is a deeply personal installation piece which expresses Hahn's memory of her grandfather on the Day of the Dead. Done with computer animated stills of her grandfather's image shifting from flesh to skull, the piece creates an eerie emotional effect. The sound track was made by mixing various sounds and voices with eight tape recorders and playing them into the microphone of a home video recorder. This *rasquache* method of working gives the sound track an unfamiliar resonance, placing emphasis on the Day of the Dead as a personal experience. *Replies of the Night* represents Hahn's personal reaction to her own cultural legacy.

Another compelling Chicana directed video is *Las mujeres de Pilsen* (*The Women of Pilsen*). The tape was made by a group of Mexican and Chicana women who live in the *barrios* of Chicago's South Side. The project director, Dálida Maria Benfield, worked with ten women to form the Oral History Project. After a brief training period, the women shot and edited a tape which presents the stories of four of the participants in the group. The look of the tape is raw, often consisting of a single long take in close up lasting for five minutes or more. The sound track includes numerous thuds from an unbalanced microphone cable. But these technical aspects do not pose any drawbacks for the viewer and, instead, add to the realism of the image, relaying a sense of urgency to the stories. The lower technical values of the tape also offer a refreshing counterpoint to the highly manipulated images seen on interview programs which plague network television.

The first interview is with a woman named María. She is a professional looking Chicana in her forties. María speaks about how her parents were *braceros* (farmworkers) who were proud of their hard working lifestyle. She does not go on to offer an analysis of the *bracero* system as oppressive but rather shifts her discussion to the topic of how she, as a contemporary Chicana, has struggled. She begins by telling how her parents saved her from marrying at a young age. The first young man she fell in love with turned out to be a murderer. The second young man she loved but broke up with ended up having twelve children. The third man she loved was very "square" she says. She knew he would please her parents, so she married him. But, as it turned out, this man, now her husband, refused to let her have the education she wanted. María says she decided to leave him and her corporate job to pursue a career which would fulfill her. She speaks of Pilsen, the *barrio*, as a good place to live. She says the people there are poor and don't pretend to be otherwise. The only problem with the neighborhood, says María, are the men.

The second interview is with Aurora who speaks in Spanish. The interviewer provides simultaneous English translation. Aurora grew up and married in Mexico. She left her husband because he was a drug addict. She came across the border with her children in the trunk of a car and lived with her relatives in Chicago. Aurora tells how she worked from 5 p.m. to 5 a.m. everyday for $3.35 an hour. She returned to Mexico when her husband died and then came back to Chicago to work. Upon her second return to Pilsen, Aurora was forced by the economic conditions of the country to leave her two oldest children behind in Mexico.

In contrast to the quiet alienation in Aurora's voice, the next subject in the tape, Diane, is young, extroverted and effervescent. Diane begins by describing how the closing of the steel mills on the South Side devastated the community and led to the development of gangs in Pilsen (due to the lack of jobs). Diane then shifts to the subject of her lesbianism. She tells us it is hard to be a lesbian in Pilsen. There are very few Chicanas who are out, and many of those who are, have been beaten up or raped by the gangs. Her tone is not bitter but rather self-assured and almost joking. Surprisingly, Diane does not resent the gangs. Instead she preaches that gangs should be mobilized to resist the outside forces which compel them to live their lives in such self-destructive ways.

The final interview is with Rosa who is framed in a two-shot with her young son in her arms. Rosa begins by saying that it is rare for women in Mexico to come to the U.S. by themselves. Women who do this are believed to end up as whores. Rosa came from Texas with her family and grew up in Chicago. She says her ways are more like the *güeros* (the whites) but that her husband is a Mexican who believes in the old ways. He will not allow her to wear shorts. When she became pregnant with his child in high school, her husband tried to force her not to finish her degree. However, her father (a Mexican who was "more like here") told her to finish high school. Rosa laments that now her husband will not let her go to college. To find fulfillment, she joined an organization of Latinas who trained her how to perform as a clown for parties and events. Though she enjoys it tremendously, Rosa notes that many other women in the neighborhood think she is crazy because they believe only men should perform as clowns.

As a whole, these four interviews present a vision of a Chicana community which is diverse and articulate. The comments of these women revolve around a common denominator of gender-based oppression. Their testimonies provide us with an organic approach to analyzing the forces which circumscribe their life choices. María and Rosa mention how the traditional values in the community held by both men and women have prevented them from seeking educations. But the

tape stops short of suggesting that moving more towards North
American values is the solution for sexism. The interview with Diane
complicates the problem further. Diane notes that the younger men in
the neighborhood (who have presumably distanced themselves from
Mexico) still abide by an abusive code of male behavior. She attributes
their actions to the worsening economic situation in Chicago. Aurora's
story confirms Diane's accusations of a flawed North American
economic structure when she tells us that she could not make enough
money to feed her children while working twelve hours a day in a
Chicago factory. In the end, *The Women of Pilsen* encourages us to see
that these women can construct an eloquent dialogue concerning the
cultural and economic forces which shape the lives of Latinas.

The final example of Chicana filmmaking which I will discuss here
is *The Devil Never Sleeps* (1994), a feature length "documystery"
written and directed by Lourdes Portillo. An accomplished independent
filmmaker, Portillo blends traditional and experimental techniques in
documentary and narrative styles in this ground-breaking documentary.
The film tells the story of Portillo's return to her birthplace in
Chihuahua, Mexico, to investigate the death of her favorite uncle,
Oscar Ruíz Almeída. Portillo narrates the story in voice over to create
an intimate account of her journey. In the process of uncovering the
bizarre circumstances surrounding her uncle's death, Portillo reveals
aspects of the Mexican psyche which shape her family and herself.

Stylistically, *The Devil Never Sleeps* vacillates between a forties'
detective film and investigative journalism. The movie opens with what
sounds like a Hollywood score. A dreamlike melody reminiscent of a
child's music box lulls us into a state of expectation. On screen,
Portillo is seated in a dark room in front of a black rotary phone, the
kind of prop one would find in a noire film. The lighting is low key.
On the voice track Portillo says, "It all started when ..." She speaks to
Oscar's wife, her Aunt Ofelia, who sounds distraught but yet
mysteriously ambivalent over the loss of her husband. With the
narrative plot cues planted, Portillo then uproots her audience and
launches into a fast paced documentary segment. She uses numerous
hand held shots of the arid landscape of the small town where she grew
up. Her voice over continues with the same dry, self-doubting wit
common to the detective genre but tempered with a bit of
rascuachismo. She tells us the story of how her uncle grew up in
poverty but she ends it with the comment that her grandmother was so

poor the only thing she was able to leave to her children when she died was her orthopedic shoes (which Portillo's aunts had bronzed). At another point, Portillo speaks of the patron saint of her home town. Santa Rita, she says, is the patron saint of boils and desperate causes. The combined attitude of reverence and irreverence in her narration extends the atmosphere of uncertainty to this Mexican world beyond fact or fiction.

Portillo's journey to Mexico takes as its central theme the filmmaker's search for the truth about aspects of her own Mexican identity. It provides her with the opportunity to confront her past and its impact on her present sense of self. She tells us, "When I dream of home, something always slips away from me, just beneath the surface." As she delves deeper into her family history, she finds the waters murky, clouded by traditions in Mexican culture that make storytelling akin to melodrama. One of the first places the filmmaker shows us in Mexico is the movie theater where she saw her first film. She explains that in Mexico history is like melodrama and reminds us of the murders of Villa, Zapata and more recently presidential candidate Colosio as examples. As the film progresses, Portillo develops her references to melodrama even further. She brings in shots of herself watching *telenovelas*. She keys images from the television screen over the lenses of her glasses and sometimes juxtaposes the juicy bits of gossip from interviews with her relatives with lines from *telenovelas* which sound strikingly similar in tone and content. A central point of Portillo's film is in her own self investigation of how she relates to this tendency to see the world as melodrama. According to the family, Oscar's life was rife with incredible highs and lows. Portillo allows us to get momentarily caught up in the drama of their telling of his story. Oscar, they say, came up from poverty to become a millionaire mayor of his town. At the pinnacle of his success, Oscar's beloved wife tragically died of cancer. The family was shocked when only two months after the first wife died, he married a young girl from a lower class, Ofelia. Later, the cruel Ofelia forced him to cut off ties with his children from his first marriage.

While Portillo maintains this gripping melodramatic storyline she periodically pulls us back out of the narrative by adding self-reflexive shots which comment on the act of interpretation. At one point, Portillo gives us an extreme close up shot of lips whispering to draw attention to gossip as a form of storytelling. Gossip is the principal form of communication in these small towns; the way life is mediated in the Mexican provinces. In another masterful sequence where Portillo's Aunt mentions that Oscar had been having an affair with Ofelia before his wife's death, Portillo cuts to a shot of a man carrying a mirror through the town. The camera is close on the mirror as the Aunt mentions that in the provinces it is acceptable for a man to have an affair as long as he is discrete and "elegant" about it. The town's reflection in the mirror, married with the Aunt's story signals that the family attitudes are symptomatic of greater cultural influences. Melodrama becomes problematized. The film argues that it is impossible to tell if the Mexican sensibility generated the *telenovela* or if the *telenovela* generated the Mexican sensibility.

As a Mexicana Portillo feels a fascination for melodrama. As a North American, she cannot accept these stories at face value and must question their power over her. Norma Alarcón mentions that Chicana theorists tend to formulate Third World feminine consciousness in terms of a weaving process. They liken Chicana identity to a tapestry of plural personalities.[26] In *The Devil Never Sleeps*, Portillo occupies a place in the narrative similar to the subject in Gloria Anzaldúa's *Borderlands/La Frontera*. She is an object of multiple indoctrinations and oppositional discourses. She is not only investigating her uncle's death but the interstices of its telling. By playing old home movies of her uncle she interrogates her own memory and the way she herself has made a myth of her uncle, her Mexico, her heritage.

Portillo's film also examines the interplay between the conventions of documentary used to create our perception of what is evidence and how that evidence creates and sustains myths. One of these myths the film contends with is the notion of *la familia*. The film begins with Portillo's romanticized memory of holidays with her beloved Uncle Oscar. She remembers him as magnetic and loving. But as the film develops, we find out that the man she idolized made his millions by polluting the lands he farmed; that he betrayed his wife and deserted his children. His close relationship with his brothers and sisters also deteriorated, and, in the end, it is revealed that the siblings are angry because he cut them out of his will. We discover that Oscar's siblings believe that his second wife used Oscar for his social status. They regard her as a low class social climber. In Portillo's scenarios, the sacred unit of the family is demystified. Love and loyalty are concepts under extreme scrutiny exposed in an ironic light as relationships

which, in the last instance, can be boiled down to purely economic
components.

At another level the film also interrogates gender stereotypes and
foregrounds the issue of gender representation. As the narrative
develops, it becomes evident that Portillo has cleverly cast her Aunt
Ofelia in the role of the femme fatale. After hearing so many evil
stories about Ofelia's social climbing, about how Ofelia beat Oscar's
first daughter and how she changed her description of the way Oscar
had died, Portillo becomes convinced that her Aunt is hiding
something. The film climaxes when Portillo tapes a phone conversation
with Ofelia. Portillo begs Ofelia to give her an interview. Ofelia brags
about how much home movie footage she has of Oscar, but refuses to
lend it to Portillo for the film. Ofelia ultimately refuses to give Portillo
permission to use her voice in the film. Portillo then undergoes a crisis
of conscience and asks a priest if it would be immoral to use the phone
conversation in the film without Ofelia's permission. We know of
course that Portillo opted to use the interview in the film. What we
don't know until we see the credits is that Ofelia's telephone
conversations were reenacted by an actor. When we see this in the
credits we must readjust our entire attitude toward the film. We ask
ourselves, why did the director stage the conversations? We are forced
to look back into the film and what we discover is a complex discourse
on the representation of powerful women. Ofelia is condemned by the
relatives because they believe she is a femme fatale. Oscar married her
thinking she was passive and could easily be controlled. Instead she
controlled him, perhaps to the point of murdering him and taking away
his fortune. Portillo shows us how factors in her personality compel
Portillo to replicate this negative image of Ofelia. Portillo's ties to
family, the appeal of melodrama and the enticement of making a great
documentary film drive her to falsify evidence and present fiction as
fact. To strengthen her melodrama, Portillo is forced to portray Ofelia
as a whining, unlikable character on the phone. But in the end Portillo
is able to undercut the negative stereotype she has set up by showing
us in the credits that it is Ofelia who has the last laugh. Ofelia controls
her own structured absence in the narrative by refusing to grant the
interview. Unlike the femme fatales of the forties who must be
punished for their acts of dominance, the powerful Ofelia gets away
with murder.

The title of the film emanates from this critique of representations
of female passivity and power. "The devil never sleeps" is a common

folk saying in Mexico. José Limón explains that the devil also haunts the popular imagination as it is expressed in Mexican American folk tales. He attributes the periodic appearance of the devil in stories of contemporary Mexican American experience to an underlying antagonism which may be at the very center of political, social and historic life of the Mexican American community.[27] This also applies to the case of gender relations. Limón studied a situation in a small Texas border town where the community claimed the devil had appeared to several young Chicanas at a local dance hall. He found that devil sightings were the cultural expression of social contradictions generated by capitalism. The traditional moral economy of the Chicano agricultural community was being threatened by the incursion of a new moral code. Advanced capitalism was bringing in a new set of social behaviors among the youth. Hence, the stories of apparitions of the devil manifested themselves as warnings against shifts in traditional value systems.

In *The Devil Never Sleeps* the traditional value systems are also called into question. Portillo shows how false notions of *la familia* inscribe her various aunts in passive roles within the family. Because Ofelia subverts the traditional hierarchical system in the Mexican family she is regarded as an evil presence. Portillo interposes her North American point of view on the situation, plays the devil's advocate and exposes gender relations as site of profound contradictions.

The range of these three Chicana films is indicative of a thriving Chicana film movement which confronts not just Anglocentrism but a wide variety of oppressions. Occupying multiple identity positions as women, as Chicanas and as people of color, Chicanas work from a vantage point of triple consciousness. Fregoso makes the point that, in essence, Chicana filmmakers accomplish what Ramón Saldívar says Chicana writers have done. Their works construct "a critique of a critique of oppression."[28] Unfortunately, Chicana productions do not circulate within the commercial distribution markets afforded to the feature filmmakers. One would hope that the Chicana filmmakers will soon break into the industry and make their impact felt in that arena.

CONCLUSION

The Hollywood social problem film as a genre dealing with Chicano protagonists has typically avoided questioning racism by proposing that Chicanos either assimilate or stay in the *barrios* without seeking empowerment. In *Only Once in a Lifetime*, the genre is reworked as blame is placed on the white characters who are portrayed as agents of a broader racist system. But the issue of assimilation is still a central part of the plot. Rather than developing this theme through the struggle of the male protagonist, the director shifts it on to a secondary character, Consuelo, who must decide whether or not to commit both their lives to helping *la raza*. Unfortunately, her decision, which could have been developed as a powerful statement on the place of Chicanas in the Movement as well as a Chicana rewriting of the social problem genre, is couched in terms of a conventional romantic melodrama. Her decision to stay becomes dependent on her desire to be with Francisco when it is implied that, if he weren't in love with her, she would never break with the traditions of *la familia*. Consequently, the gender bias which is introduced through the love story undercuts the progressive discourse on social problems. This calls into question the appropriateness of using unaltered genre forms and suggests that filmmakers look at the counter-aesthetic practices of the NLACM and of Chicana directors for new modes of expression.

NOTES

1. The films are: *Bordertown* (1935), *A Medal for Benny* (1945), *The Lawless* (1950), *Right Cross* (1950), *My Man and I* (1952), *The Ring* (1952), *Salt of the Earth* (1954), *Trial* (1955), *Giant* (1956), and *Requiem for a Heavyweight* (1962).

2. Chon Noriega, "Citizen Chicano: The Trials and Titillations of Ethnicity in the American Cinema, 1935-1962," *Social Research* 58 (Summer 1991): 413.

3. Ibid., p. 428.

4. For an in depth account of Mexican immigration policy in the U.S. consult, Juan Ramón García, *Operation Wetback: The Mass Deportation of Mexican Undocumented Workers in 1954* (Westport, Conn.: Greenwood Press,

1980) and Patricia Morgan, *Shame of a Nation: A Documented Story of Police-State Terror Against Mexican Americans in the U.S.A.* (Los Angeles: Los Angeles Committee for Protection of the Foreign Born, 1954).

5. Betty García-Bahne, "La Chicana and the Chicano Family," in *Essays on La Mujer*, ed. Rosaura Sanchez (Los Angeles: Chicano Studies Center Publications, 1977), pp. 44 - 45.

6. From Rodolfo "Corky" Gonzáles, "What Political Road for the Chicano Movement," *The Militant* (March 30, 1970; reprinted in *A Documentary History of the Mexican Americans*, ed. Wayne Moquin and Charles Van Doren, (New York: Praeger Publishers, 1971), p. 488.

7. Sonia A. López, "The Role of the Chicana within the Student Movement," in *Essays on La Mujer*, ed. Rosaura Sanchez (Los Angeles: University of California Press, 1977), pp. 16 - 29.

8. Jennie V. Chavez, "An Opinion: Women of the Mexican American Movement," *Mademoiselle* 74 (April 1972), p. 82.

9. Alfredo Mirandé, "Chicano Fathers: Response and Adaptation to Emergent Roles," Working Paper Series No. 13, (Stanford: Stanford Center for Chicano Research, 1986).

10. Christine Gledhill, "The Melodramatic Field: An Investigation," in *Home is Where the Heart Is: Studies in Melodrama and the Woman's Film*, ed. Christine Gledhill (London: BFI, 1987), pp. 5 -43.

11. See Elayne Rapping's *Rapping on Soaps* distributed by Paper Tiger Television on video tape and also Jean Franco, "The Incorporation of Women: A Comparison of North American and Mexican Popular Narrative in *Studies in Entertainment: Critical Approaches to Mass Culture*, ed. Tania Modleski (Bloomington: Indiana University Press, 1986), pp. 119-138.

12. Ana López, "The Melodrama in Latin America: Films, Telenovelas and the Currency of a Popular Form," *Wideangle* 7, (Fall 1988): 5-13.

13. Some 65 tapes were produced, most of those by Jesús Salvador Treviño and Eduardo Moreno for KCET-TV, Los Angeles.

14. See Catherine Saalfield and Ray Navarro, "Not Just Back and White: AIDS Media and People of Color," *Centro Bulletin* 2 (Spring 1990): 70 -78.

15. Mary Ann Doane, *The Desire to Desire: The Woman's Film of the 1940's* (Bloomington: Indiana University Press, 1987).

16. Ibid., p. 109.

17. Norma Cantú, "Women, Then and Now: An Analysis of the Adelita Image versus the Chicana a Political Writer and Philosopher," in *Chicana Voices: Intersections of Class, Race and Gender*, ed. Teresa Córdova, Norma Cantú, Gilberto Cárdenas, Juan García and Christine M. Sierra (Austin: The Center for Mexican American Studies, 1986), pp. 8 - 11.

18. Adelaída Del Castillo, "Malintzín Tenepal: A Preliminary Look into a New Perspective," in *Essays on La Mujer* (Los Angeles: University of California Press, 1977), pp. 124-150.

19. Octavio Paz, *The Labyrinth of Solitude, Life and Thought in Mexico*, trans. Lysander Kemp (New York: Random House, 1961).

20. Tania Modleski, "Time and Desire in the Woman's Film," *Cinema Journal* 23, (Spring 1984): 26-27.

21. See Noriega, "Citizen Chicano" for a discussion of biracial romance in the social problem film.

22. Rosa Linda Fregoso writes about the use of the white woman in Chicano film as emblematic of Chicano desire for social mobility. See Rosa Linda Fregoso, *The Bronze Screen*, pg. 51.

23. Rosa Linda Fregoso, "Chicana Film Practices," pp. 189-205.

24. Fregoso points out that no real consideration of Chicana film/video was shown in the programming of the recent film series that was part of the "Chicano Art: Resistance and Affirmation" exhibit at the Wight Gallery in Los Angeles. Chicanas were also excluded from "Chicanos 90" a film series hosted by Mexican President Salinas de Gortari. Rosa Linda Fregoso, "Close Encuentro of a First Kind: The Cruzando Fronteras Conference," *The Independent* 14 (May 1991): 13-16.

25. For a discussion of Chicana productions see Rosa Linda Fregoso, *The Bronze Screen*, pp. 93-121.

26. Norma Alarcón, "The Theoretical Subject(s) of *This Bridge Called My Back* and Anglo-American Feminism," in *Criticism in the Borderlands: Studies in Chicano Literature, Culture and Ideology*, eds. Héctor Calderón and José David Saldívar (Durham: Duke University Press, 1991), pp. 28-43.

27. José E. Limón, "Dancing with the Devil: Society, Gender, and the Political Unconscious in Mexican-American South Texas," in *Criticism in the Borderlands: Studies in Chicano Literature, Culture, and Ideology*, eds. Héctor Calderón and José David Saldívar (Durham: Duke University Press, 1991), pp. 221-236.

28. Ramón Saldívar, *Chicano Narrative: The Dialectics of Difference* (Madison: University of Wisconsin Press, 1990), p. 173.

VI

TRANS-CREATIVE STRATEGIES OF CHICANO MAINSTREAM CINEMA

> When John Smith—an immigrant, after all—arrived
> in Jamestown, Pocahontas began to be ethnic.
>
> —Mary Dearborn[1]

There is an inseparable relationship between ethnic expression and the dominant culture. The situation requires that the ethnic director serve as mediator of the dominant and the minority discourses. As one prominent Chicano critic puts it:

> . . . you cannot talk about minority cultures without a
> considerable amount of reference to the majority culture .
> . . you have to take the majority culture into account. This
> is a process already familiar to us from studies of
> American slavery, whether in the United States or Latin
> America. The slave has to know the master better than the
> master knows the slave. It seems to me that Chicano
> writers have always understood American culture very
> well.[2]

Chicano feature filmmakers are situated within a similar dialectical relationship to the majority culture. As we have seen from the analysis of each of the films, Chicano cinema borrows, adapts, confronts and, in some instances, transforms dominant Hollywood cinema into a new ethnic aesthetic practice. This cinema practice comments on Chicano marginalization while at the same time creating a meta-discourse on negative representations of Chicanos propagated by mainstream cinema. Understood in this sense, Chicano cinema can be defined not merely in terms of an ethnic continuum which posits oppositional elements against assimilationist ones but more appropriately, as a "trans-creative" cinema.

The concept behind trans-creation was derived from the theories of the Border Arts Workshop. It defines Latino cultural production as a fusion between many cultures in a continual process of hybridization. The term, itself, was coopted from bilingual advertising language by scholars Juan Flores and George Yúdice who have reappropriated it to describe the phenomenon of Border Art:

> Latino self-formation as trans-creation—to "trans-create" the term beyond its strictly commercialist coinage—is more than a culture of resistance, or it is "resistance" and more than the sense of standing up against concerted hegemonic domination. It confronts the prevailing ethos by congregating an ethos of its own, not necessarily an outright adversarial but certainly an alternative ethos. The Latino border trans-creates the impinging dominant cultures by constituting the space for their free intermingling—free because it is dependent on neither, nor on the reaction of one to the other for its own legitimacy.[3]

The significance of envisioning Chicano cinema as trans-creative is in its critical break from older conceptions of ethnic cinemas as pure negation of false differences supported by the status quo. Rather than determining ethnicity in terms of difference as it is defined by the dominant culture, trans-creative cinema interrogates the notion of ethnic difference in a totally new light. Trans-creative Chicano cinema exposes the elements of the dominant culture which work at leveling contexts and expectations. It uncovers the details of Chicano identity without resorting to what Trinh T. Minh-ha calls a "simplicity of essences."[4]

The film *Cambio* (*Change* 1994) is a pivotal Chicano production which exemplifies a trans-creative approach to Chicano filmmaking. The first Chicano feature to be produced in Chicago, *Cambio* tells the story of how three Chicano families come to terms with each other's expectations of what it means to be Mexican American. (In Chicago,

most people of Mexican heritage call themselves Mexican Americans.)
Director Juan Frausto begins the narrative from the perspective of José,
an aspiring writer who is being pressured by his father to either go to
college or get a job. The story opens as José's aunt, uncle and cousin,
Rafael, come from Tijuana to visit for a few weeks. José takes Rafael
to visit their other cousin Rogelio. We see that José disapproves of
Rogelio because Rogelio's family has money and tries to distance
themselves from José's more working class family. Rogelio and his
mother want to assimilate into North American culture. Rogelio has
changed his name to Roger and has applied for American citizenship.

During the era of Chicano nationalism, one could have predicted
the ending to this story. The righteous José would berate Rogelio into
seeing that he had become *agringado* and a snob. Rogelio would
eventually forsake his ambitions to assimilate and return to his Mexican
roots. But in *Cambio*, Frausto has seen fit to interject a much more
complex explanation of *Chicanismo*. He focuses on the problems of
straddling multiple cultures. He establishes parameters of identity which
are fluid and inclusive. Rafael, the cousin from Mexico, is a character
who grew up in Chicago and seems comfortable in both countries.
Rafael has achieved a spiritual balance between North and South and
projects the sense of self-knowledge which José is searching for.

Frausto uses the character of Rafael to structure the film from
multiple points of view. He has scenes in which Rafael meets with José
and Rogelio individually. The audience sees the strengths and flaws in
the way the two Chicanos position themselves in relation to Rafael and
how they view their heritage, their future and each other. During
Rafael's conversation with Rogelio, the audience discovers that Rogelio
resents José because he has dropped out of college, does not have a job
and dresses like a working class Mexican. José, on the other hand,
despises Rogelio for wanting to fit into U.S. society and for rejecting
his Mexican heritage.

The film reaches its climax when Rogelio's father is arrested. The
father had been working with José's father, selling false I.D.'s to
immigrants. Rogelio assumes that his uncle was jealous of their wealth
and, thus, was the one who reported him to the police. When the
vengeful Rogelio picks up the phone to report his uncle to the
authorities, Rogelio's mother stops him and reveals that Rogelio's
father was actually arrested for dealing drugs. The scene turns the
audience against Rogelio, showing he and his father to be of low moral

standards because they have placed their allegiance to the dollar over the *dignidad* of the family.

But just when it appears that justice has been served by the downfall of this branch of the family which has forsaken its roots and blindly assimilated, Frausto disrupts things, challenging nationalist estimations of right and wrong. Frausto cuts to a scene in which José tells Rafael that he is glad Rogelio's father was caught and believes it to be a deserved punishment for Rogelio's arrogant *agringado* ways. Instead of agreeing, Rafael confronts José, telling him to make amends with his cousin and with his own conscience. He counsels José not to over-identify with Mexico at the risk of denying aspects of his personality which are uniquely North American. Rafael tells José that he sometimes admires things in the United States. José is taken aback by this statement and is forced to come to terms with his own estimation of himself. In the end, José makes amends with Rogelio and reevaluates his sense of identity.

At the end of the film, Rogelio also goes through a change. When his father comes home on bond, his father tells Rogelio that he sold drugs to finance Rogelio's lavish lifestyle. Rogelio realizes that he will have to make economic sacrifices and resolves to also come to terms with his Mexican heritage. Rogelio's mother has a change of heart as well, and, in the final scene, joins her sister to visit her relatives in Tijuana.

Cambio presents an interesting counter-vision of nationalistic views of identity, especially in its refusal to romanticize the part of the family who lives in Mexico. Rafael's family is economically stable. They own a video store in Tijuana, speak English well and, having lived in the U.S. previously, are comfortable with U.S. culture. The three cousins were born in Mexico and spent their childhoods there. But they have also spent many years in Chicago. Therefore, there is little sense of otherness associated with Mexico. Rather, *Cambio* creates a refreshing realism that emphasizes the familiar to such an extent that the notion of difference is called into question. The film also extends the Chicano cultural identity debate across the border back into Mexico, suggesting that every Mexican is a potential Chicano.[5] Thus, Frausto constructs an alternative ethos, remapping identity and recontextualizing the Chicano Cinema Movement in a trans-creative mode of expression.

DESTABILIZING DIFFERENCE

Flores and Yúdice note that there has been a "paradigm shift" in ethnic theory. They see the new paradigm as *multiculturalism* and describe how multicultural works of Border Art evince the "power of the outrageous," displaying the imagination needed to "turn the historical and cultural tables."[6] *Born in East L.A.* offers one of the most effective examples of Chicano feature filmmaking which challenges the dominant culture's structuring of ethnicity. Using a *rasquache* approach to develop its discourse on Chicano ethnicity at the border, *Born in East L.A.* is an example of multicultural art. The film sets up as its central conflict Rudy's dilemma of proving his identity. His introspective journey is initiated when he is sent to the opposite side of the border to view himself and his country in terms of otherness. His confrontation with his own American attitudes leads to a dismantling of the binary system of identity coding, tearing down the *official* language of the border that designates "legal" from "illegal" and native from non-native. In the end, the national project of border maintenance appears ridiculous, and patently oppressive.

In the Cheech and Chong films, Marin exaggerates derogatory character traits to the point where the filmic style becomes obvious parody. He targets Anglos as an "ethnic" group, refiguring them as "others" so that the audience might question the whole schema of ethnic categories. In these films, Marin turns ethnicity into a set of floating signifiers. But he does not do this in an apolitical postmodernist sense. Marin's playful treatment of ethnicity goes beyond the ethnic ambiguity and "depthlessness" symptomatic of postmodernist cinema.[7] There is no decentered Chicano subjectivity in Marin's movies. His films presuppose Chicano agency. The parody is based on Chicano specific references to *pachuco/cholo* subculture. Therefore, one can conclude that the Cheech and Chong films are not an exercise in self-effacement or self-hatred but rather an outgrowth of a joking tradition and part of a Chicano history of resistance to social domination and forced separations.

What Marin and many of the other Chicano filmmakers have done is to rewrite the official discourse on ethnicity. Their movies attempt to expose racist institutional systems by highlighting contradictions. They also challenge the textual treatment of ethnicity in mainstream cinema as they destabilize genres that hide contradictions from scrutiny.

Many of these Chicano films attempt to negotiate boundaries in such a way that they might wrest control of identifying labels and create new categories. Because of this, the border has become a thematic locus for Chicano filmmakers.

The border aesthetic developed through Chicano films is comprised of a set of culturally derived techniques. One of these techniques, the *barrio* aesthetic, offers Chicano filmmakers an alternative to Hollywood aesthetics of fantasy and illusionism by replicating the realities of everyday life of Chicano neighborhoods. Particularly influenced by this Chicano sensibility is the film *Raíces de sangre*. In *Raíces de sangre*, Jesús Salvador Treviño creates a nationalist allegory which preaches the necessity of all Chicanos to return to the *barrios* to work for the good of the community. The *barrio* as a working class space is juxtaposed with corrupt influences of the capitalist wealth which tempt the protagonist, Carlos, away from his heritage. Through the character of Carlos, Treviño equates Chicano nationalism with a hemispheric consciousness and the struggles of other Third World peoples against imperialism. From Treviño's perspective, immigration is analyzed in terms of international revolution. Hence, we find that in *Raíces de sangre* an internationalist perspective is superimposed on nationalism. The *barrio* is not just a local space but a geopolitical starting point—a site of multiple struggles. These struggles begin at the level of the individual conscience, expand to include the plight of the community and then continue on to encompass a broader Pan-Latin American struggle.

The internationalist influences on Chicano filmmakers came from both an exposure by Chicano political activists to independence movements occurring world wide and the alliances built between Chicano filmmakers and the New Latin American Cinema Movement (NLACM). Treviño and Artenstein's work falls almost directly in line with a Pan-Latin American cultural agenda which poses an alternative to U.S. imperialism and their internationalism also necessarily invokes the premise of class struggle. *Raíces de sangre* takes this position by extending its narrative across the border to form a story that poses the plight of Chicanos and Mexicans as a common one which must be solved by an international worker's revolution.

Break of Dawn marries the issue of class-based oppression with the struggle for Spanish language rights. The film delineates Spanish usage as a progressive characteristic of *Chicanismo*. Spanish creates a public sphere in the film and symbolically drapes the people on both sides of the border under a common mantle of Latino identity. This linguistic unity is presented as oppositional to the status quo by virtue of the fact that it is linked with the music of the Mexican Revolution (which was an anti-imperialist war in many respects) and because it is an indirect reference to the current Latino struggle against the English-only Movement. In this way, *Break of Dawn* very cleverly situates an internationalist, anti-imperialist agenda *within* the borders of the U.S.—a country which has, through colonialist-like aggression, caused multiple Latino identities to become collective as a survival strategy within and beyond U.S. borders.

By dealing with *Chicanismo* as a dialectic among indigenous, "American" and Third World identities, the films often do what Cornel West says progressive internationalist culture should do, "Address history as in part the cross-fertilization of a variety of different cultures, usually under conditions of hierarchy."[8] The fact that these films are mainstream commercialized products does not diminish their potential oppositionality to racist and class-based constructions of ethnicity. The alternative nature of these films seems to depend more on the way a particular mainstream structuring device is "trans-created" than whether or not a technique is used or not used. Nevertheless, it should be reiterated that while the majority of these films are highly politicized, their challenge to dominant constructions of ethnic identities is often weakened by the absence of other discourses that now appear in Chicano art such as gender construction, sexual preference and regional concerns, among others.

Textual weaknesses in Chicano films surface when Chicano subjectivity is not presented as nuanced and diverse within a Chicano context. Along these lines, Rosaura Sánchez comments on the importance of developing a multi-faceted, inclusionary view of Chicano identity:

> Defining Chicano culture . . . not only assumes a homogeneous, uniform ethnic identity, but also posits a single subject position. What is ignored in this search for identity is not only the heterogeneity of the population, but the fact that this ethnic scheme fits well within the larger framework of hegemonical ideological discourses used deftly to manipulate us, not only by pitting us against other

marginalized ethnic groups, but also by having us posit
ethnicity or culture as the major or only problem.[9]

This problem of essentializing Chicano subjectivity as a masculine
identity played havoc with the progressive impulses in the film *Once in
a Lifetime*. The film failed to validate the agency of the Chicana
character by positioning her crucial decision to stay in East Los
Angeles in terms other than her dedication to the community. Instead,
her choice to stay in the *barrio* was premised on her love for the
protagonist, Domínguez. Opting to structure the film within the
boundaries of the romance genre led the director to position the
Chicana character as a passive subject in the narrative. As a result of
the gender bias *Only Once in a Lifetime* undermined the progressive
anti-assimilationist statement attempted by the rewriting of the social
problem genre. *Only Once in a Lifetime* exemplifies the need for
Chicano filmmakers to rethink essentializing genre structures before
incorporating them into their work.

TACTICS OF THE UNDERDOG

In 1992, twenty three year old Chicano filmmaker Robert
Rodriguez became one of the most sought after directors in Hollywood.
He was signed to develop two films for Columbia Pictures after studio
executives screened his seven thousand dollar feature film, *El Mariachi*.
The rights to the film were also picked up by Columbia who paid
Rodriguez to recut *El Mariachi* and prepare the subtitles for a 35 mm
release print.

Rodriguez originally produced *El Mariachi* with the intent of selling
it to the ultra low budget straight-to-video Spanish home video market.
Since he'd been a teenager Rodriguez had been making movies with a
home video camera and editing them on the fly with two consumer
model VHS decks. He had won several awards for his short videos and
used them to convince a Dean at the University of Texas at Austin to
let him study filmmaking there. As a summer project to sharpen his
filmmaking skills, Rodriguez decided to shoot a feature with an old
high school friend of his, Carlos Gallardo. Rodriquez and Gallardo had
spent summers in Gallardo's home town of Ciudad Acuña in northern
Mexico video taping shorts and the two were confident they could use

locations in the town as sets in their feature. Rodriguez borrowed a 16 mm camera and a Marantz tape recorder (which does not run on crystal sync). He shot the film by himself without a crew and then edited it on 3/4 inch video tape at a local cable access station.[10]

Rodriguez and Gallardo had gotten the idea to produce a low budget action film for the Spanish straight-to-video market while visiting the set of *Like Water for Chocolate* (directed by Alfonso Arau, 1992) which was being shot in Ciudad Acuña the spring of 1991. The production manager of *Like Water* had seen one of Rodriguez' shorts and offered him an unpaid position to direct an action film budgeted at $30,000. Rodriguez turned down the offer because he decided he could make his own film and keep the profits. Rodriguez raised $7000 to make his feature which he expected to be less than a masterpiece. He regarded the project as a chance to make some money and sharpen his filmmaking skills. What he ended up with was what he has called "a blow-off Spanish home video mexploitation flick."[11]

The Mexican film industry had not always been a purveyor of cheap action material. Throughout the '30s and '40s the film industry in Mexico was a source of national pride, producing westerns, comedies and musicals that were seen all over Latin America. However, after the 1950s a downward spiral began which culminated in the dissolution of the nationalized film industry in Mexico. By the eighties and nineties the bulk of Mexican films were made by unskilled financiers and released to the home video market. Most of these tapes fall into one of two categories—cheap sex comedies or relentless shoot-'em-ups with titles like *Perros Rabiosos* (*Rabid Dogs*) and *Perros Rabiosos 2* (*Rabid Dogs 2*). In his book about the making of *El Mariachi*, Rodriguez comments on how poorly made these Mexican home videos are produced and mentions hearing the Spanish market video distributors admit to the low quality of their products.[12]

By using the cheap action genre Rodriguez was plugging into a vehicle of mass culture which makes no pretensions about itself. Nevertheless, the prevalence of genre in Mexican culture has lead the entrenched Mexican intelligentsia to condemn these mexploitation films as contaminated cultural products and attribute their popularity to the corruptive tendencies of transnational capitalism. They believe a collapse of national culture has been brought on by Mexico's shift to global consumerism. Their dismissive view of mass culture is founded on a nostalgic aspiration for unalienated modes of life, for a national "authenticity." But a new generation of Mexican and Latin American cultural critics refuse to see mass culture as a mere copy of "First World" commodities. Instead they have put forth concepts such as "transculturation,"[13] and "cultural reconversion,"[14] to delineate ways diverse communities in Latin America mediate culture under global capitalism. These theories are similar to Jesús Martín-Barbero's rearticulation of *lo popular*, but differ in that they do not speak so much to the oppositional tendencies of popular art but rather they address the protean nature of Latin American culture under transnational capital. Like the process of transcreation in U.S. Latino art, reconversion incorporates the inevitability of developing coping strategies to transfer patrimony of new media back into the hands of Southern Hemisphere cultural producers. According to Néstor García Canclini, in Latin America there is reconversion by hegemonic groups and also by the popular classes. In both sectors cultural workers adapt their knowledge and traditional practices to new circumstances:

> In most cases, the difficulties of survival reduce this adaptation to a pragmatic and commercial apprenticeship, although younger generations increasingly redraw the boundaries between traditional and modern, local and foreign, popular and elite.[15]

While these theories of cultural reconversion do not deal directly with the phenomenon of the mexploitation film they can provide a useful framework for contextualizing *El Mariachi* in relation to mexploitation. *El Mariachi* is the story of an itinerant guitarist who wanders into a town looking for work and is mistaken for a drug dealer. The dealer, a Mexican called Azul, is being hunted by his former partner, an Anglo dealer named Moco. The Anglo has cheated Azul out of his share of the drug money and sends his men to gun down Azul in jail. Azul escapes and kills Moco's men in revenge. Moco resolves to have his men assassinate Azul. However, Moco's men confuse Azul with the Mariachi because both carry guitar cases and wear black. Of course, the contents of the cases differ. Azul's case contains an automatic weapon—an instrument of mass destruction—while the Mariachi's case contains an acoustic guitar—the instrument of his ancestors.

Rodriguez noted in an interview that with *El Mariachi* he wanted to make a *Road Warrior* type film in which a guy comes to town and ends up blowing the whole place up.[16] In setting the script around the story of the Mexican drug culture Rodriguez is certainly tapping into this idiom of hyper-violent entertainment characteristic of the Hollywood action film and the mexploitation genre. Yet he is also drawing on elements of the action/exploitation genre which go beyond the use of violence as pure effect.

In many ethnic action films, violence by an ethnic protagonist is represented as a means of self-defense or as a way of achieving justice in a society which bars minorities from redressing injustice in the legal sphere. In black action films, violence as a narrative technique does not always serve to exploit an African American audience hungry for a heroic vision of itself. Mark Reid points out that black action films appeal to a range of black spectatorship with differing levels of black empowerment.[17] Certain black action films create mythic heros of drug dealers and pimps by reclaiming them from a revolutionary perspective. Rodriguez intended to create his own Latino action hero with the character of *El Mariachi*. He cast his hero in the role of a mariachi because "it is the wimpiest character in Mexican culture."[18] The Mariachi grows into the hero as he is forced to eventually kill the drug king pin, Moco. Through a series of ironic circumstances, the Mariachi comes to rid the Mexican town of this Anglo gangster, realigning the balance of power towards the Mexican side of the border.

In his discussion of the crisis in contemporary Latin American culture, George Yúdice explains that the reconversion of culture in Latin America is only one facet of a larger series of daily survival strategies developed during the current period of transnational capitalism. These strategies include the formation of informal economies of legal and illegal activities which emerge to combat the unequal distribution of income and the hyperinflation brought on by "First World" exploitation. When the state participates in and, by virtue of its participation, institutionalizes illegal activities these "strategies for survival" are transformed into "permanent strategies of life."[19] The instances of drug scandals which have touched the Presidencies of Reagan and Bush (the Iran Contra scandal), President Semper in Colombia and President Salinas in Mexico provide ample evidence of the institutionalization of narcotraffic on both continents. Narcotraffic is currently the largest sector of the informal economy in Latin America. As such, Yúdice contends that narcotraffic "in its current transnational cartel form (another recent development that owes something to CIA dealings in the region) is a grotesque (and fitting) parody of capitalist corporate culture."[20]

Rodriguez' venture into what he calls mexploitation can be understood as a cinematic parody of this narcotraffic parody of corporate capitalism and an ironic commentary on the struggle for survival in Latin American. In the film, the town is run by the Anglo drug dealer. The Mexican residents of Acuña resent him, not because he sells drugs, but because he is a bastard *extranjero* (foreigner) who won't share part of the business with the citizenry. In Rodriguez' action film, the informal economy is a way of life in Acuña. The evil in *El Mariachi* is not the existence of drugs in the town, it is the presence of the Anglo businessman who insists on monopoly control of drug sales. To please his audience, Rodriguez provides his Mexican viewers with a nationalist parody of the Mexican stereotype of corporate North America. The scenes with Moco create a villain one loves to hate. His lines are pronounced with a heavy Anglo accent and delivered in a stylized, overbearing manner. Rodriguez dresses Moco in a white cotton suit and straw hat reminiscent of a turn of the century Victorian colonizer. Moco is frequently shown lounging at pool side shunning the affections of a beautiful Mexican woman. Through these scenes, Moco becomes every pompous Anglo tourist that visits Club Med. As he lights a match on the beard of one of his Mexican hired guns, Moco becomes a parody of the corporate conqueror invading Mexico to exploit her people.

As a complement to Moco's character, there is Azul who Rodriguez delineates as the parody of the homegrown Mexican working man. Azul dresses in a leather vest, jeans and cowboy boots—the garb of the northern Mexican working class. He is dark skinned and rugged. Rodriguez shows him in the opening scene, inside a cell which has no beds or toilet, just a big wooden desk and a cellular phone where Azul is sitting busily conducting his drug sales. Azul is merely a businessman trying to make a buck. But when Moco sends his men to kill Azul (i.e. muscle him out of his sales territory permanently), Azul shows he can play at Moco's own game. In a parody of the mexploitation image of the "tough guy/super macho" Rodriguez shows Azul forcing Moco to listen to the dying screams of Moco's hit men through his cellular phone. In another parody of violence, Rodriguez shows Azul returning to the bar where he has just murdered four of

Moco's men in order to pay his beer tab. At one point in the film the parody of violence evolves into the ridiculous as Moco and Azul argue over exactly how many of Moco's men Azul has killed. In the final scenes, Rodriguez has us identify with Azul. When Azul confronts Moco, he condemns Moco for the killings and says all he wanted was his money. Moco, the Anglo without a conscience, blows away both Azul and Domino (the mariachi's girlfriend). The mariachi arrives and kills Moco, fulfilling his destiny as the new Mexican enforcer. The experience transforms the Mariachi into a killer. In a parody of the ending of *The Terminator*, the Mariachi rides off on his motorcycle with a dog, a gun and a memory of the past. Through its ending, *El Mariachi* generates a parodic deconstruction of the pathology of the informal economy under late capitalism. The highly stressful way of life brought on by the system of narcotraffic is exaggerated to the point where the irrationality of violence becomes rational. Violence protects the society from the outside aggressor but at the same time transforms the traditional elements of the culture into something other.

It's interesting that Rodriguez says he was inspired by the film *Road Warrior*. The movie is about a society in which national law no longer exists. It is the holocaust at the climax of transnational capitalism. The ultra violence of the drug culture referred to in *El Mariachi* provides an apt parallel to this social decay depicted in *Road Warrior*. Like the road warrior character, El Mariachi is a moral man who must provide justice to a society in a state of flux. He is a generic Latino everyman who finds himself caught in a moment in history where he must redefine himself and his society.

In *El Mariachi* Rodriguez takes apart the Hollywood action genre and recreates it for a Mexican market. In this context as a Mexican exploitation film *El Mariachi* parodies the struggle for survival that generates the informal economy in Latin America under transnational capitalism. But *El Mariachi* also works at another level. The film was not originally sold to a Spanish home video distributor, but was picked up by Columbia Pictures and was distributed with subtitles in theaters throughout the United States. It was applauded by mainstream critics as a masterpiece. Because of this unanticipated shift in distribution channels *El Mariachi* was elevated in the minds of the U.S. audience and critics from mexploitation to innovative independent Chicano feature.

In its context as a Chicano feature, *El Mariachi* provides one of the best examples of *rascuache* cinema by a Chicano filmmaker. The circumstances of production brought on by the $7000 budget forced Rodriguez to develop coping strategies that lead to stylistic choices. Rodriguez uses quick paced editing and frequently cuts away during dialogue sequences in *El Mariachi* to cover up bad shots or losses in synch due to the fact that he could only afford to do single takes and did not record sound on an expensive Nagra sync audio recorder. His frequent use of slow motion in the film was not an homage to Sam Peckinpah but rather a way to extend the running time of the shots and a way to make his cheap bullet effects look more interesting.[21] He used the turtle in the first shots with the mariachi because the turtle happened to be at the side of the road, and the pit bull became a character because it belonged to one of the actors. Thus, much of the look of the film was inspired by the financial constraints which forced Rodriguez to make do with his low budget equipment and unpaid talent.

Tomás Ybarra-Frausto has noted that the underdog sensibility that makes up the practice of *rascuachismo* focuses on the *habla* of Chicano culture—the vernacular aspects of cultural expression.[22] *Rascuachismo* uses parodic forms rooted in Chicano culture to challenge the notion of an elaborated language and calls into question official discourse on identity, tradition and social power. Ybarra-Frausto stresses that the "hidden goal of *rascuachismo* . . . is overcoming the fear of using the tools of irony in order to gain empowerment."[23] Through its use of *rascuache* techniques *El Mariachi* creates its own *habla* of Chicano filmmaking. Rodriguez has spoken out against the waste that goes into making a big budget film.[24] He insists on working with lower budget projects to retain creative control and a more innovative look. Because his lack of funds forced him to be his own crew for *El Mariachi*, Rodriguez could improvise without risk of running over budget. The effect on the end product was to produce a film with a strong sense of location. For instance, while shooting one day Rodriguez ran into a coconut vendor. He got several shots of the vender and incorporated the bit of border realism into the movie. Rodriguez let the environment and the community of Acuña inspire the plot. In this way, the everyday aspect of the border community grounded the aesthetic choices. Also because he is Chicano and not Mexican, Rodriguez could use his position as outsider to enrich his images of Mexico with a sense of humor. The movie includes a clever scene in the bar where the mariachi first goes to ask for a job. The bartender berates the naive guitarist who says he will work for free. The bartender quips; why would he want a single guitar player when he can have an entire band. Rodriguez then pans to a scene in fast motion of a Mexican musician awaking from his siesta and rushing to play an electric keyboard. The keyboard music he makes is a mixture of Mexican folk with a bad rap beat. When he's done with the demonstration, he puts his *sombrero* over his eyes and falls back to sleep. Rodriguez creates a clash of cultural signs, a pastiche which combines the bankrupt image of the lazy Mexican with its audio equivalent. In the scene, Rodriguez undermines the utopian notion that new technology can give everyone the power to create. Through his parody of the mariachi he shows that technology can crush traditional elements of the culture by replacing it with a commodified sound which is only a bad replica of the original.

The insistent use of parody in *El Mariachi*, like in other Chicano films, should be differentiated from the way the recurrent use of parody, pastiche and irony is explained in postmodern discourse. *Rascuachismo* is not evidence of a cultural nihilism or a fracturing of subjectivity. The parodic tendencies of Chicano filmmaking rather betray the self-confident stance of the minority director in the face of the dominant culture. *El Mariachi* uses parody on many levels. It pokes fun at the representation of violence in action films, and at another level it parodies the drug culture which is itself an ironic commentary on the survival strategies which thrive under the economic world order. Parody is Rodriguez' cultural tool which allows for not the mere recycling of Hollywood forms but the ability to transcreate them. Through the appropriation of elements of Hollywood production and distribution structures Rodriguez is able to actualize the underdog sensibility and revitalize the deteriorating action genres of Hollywood and Mexico.

In conclusion, Chicano mainstream cinema is a body of work which should be understood within a new multicultural aesthetic paradigm. Instead of aiming to create an ethnic nationalist anti-Hollywood cinema tradition, these Chicano filmmakers have shown they have an affinity for certain aspects of Hollywood and its ability to reach mainstream audiences. These filmmakers use transcreative cinematic practices that incorporate techniques of border aesthetics to pry open the larger culture and interrogate its representations of ethnicity. Through their appropriation of newly constituted expressive terrains, these Chicano filmmakers are popularizing a progressive Chicano identity and are establishing a new sphere for an alternative public discourse.

NOTES

1. Mary Dearborn, *Pocahontas' Daughters* (New York: Oxford University Press, 1986), p. 17.

2. Statement by Raymund A. Paredes, June 1988 as quoted in Angie Chabram, "Chicano Critical Discourse: An Emerging Cultural Practice," *Aztlán: A Journal of Chicano Studies* 18 (1989): 77.

3. Juan Flores and George Yúdice, "Living Borders/Buscando America: Languages of Latino Self-formation," *Social Text: Theory/Culture/Ideology* 8 (Spring, 1990): 74.

4. Trinh T. Minh-ha, "Not You/Like You: Post-Colonial Woman and the Interlocking Questions of Identity and Difference," *Framework* 23, (Fall 1990), p. 72.

5. Tomás Ybarra-Frausto has noted that Mexico began to recognize the Chicano Movement and the potential that every Mexican may be a Chicano after the 1968 massacre of student protesters in Tlatelolco, Mexico City. Tomás Ybarra-Frausto, "Interview with Tomás Ybarra-Frausto: The Chicano Movement in a Multicultural/Multinational Society" in *On Edge: The Crisis in Contemporary Latin American Culture*, eds. George Yúdice, Jean Franco and Juan Flores (Minneapolis: University of Minnesota Press, 1992), p. 211.

6. Flores and Yúdice, "Living Borders," p. 79.

7. Vivian Sobchack discusses the dispersal and devaluation of ethnic specificity that leads to dangerous denial of discrimination in current Hollywood films. See her "Postmodern Modes of Ethnicity," in *Unspeakable Images: Ethnicity and the American Cinema*, ed. Lester Friedman (Urbana: University of Illinois Press, 1991), pp. 329-352.

8. Cornel West, "Diverse New World," *Democratic Left* 19 (July/August, 1991): 7.

9. Rosaura Sánchez, "Postmodernism and Chicano Literature," *Aztlán: A Journal of Chicano Studies* 18 (Fall, 1987): 8.

10. For a full account of Rodriguez' experiences directing the movie see Robert Rodriguez, *Rebel Without a Crew: Or How a 23-Year-Old Filmmaker with $7,000 Became a Hollywood Player* (New York: Penguin, 1995).

11. Ibid., p. 150.

12. Ibid., p. 79.

13. Angel Rama, *Transculturacíon narrativa in América Latina*, (México: Siglo XXI, 1982).

14. Néstor García Canclini, "Cultural Reconversion" in *On Edge: The Crisis in Contemporary Latin American Culture*, eds. George Yúdice, Jean Franco and Juan Flores (Minneapolis: University of Minnesota Press, 1992), pp. 29-43.

15. Ibid., p. 38.

16. Rustin Thompson, "The Reformation of a Rebel Without a Crew," *Movie Maker Magazine* 15 (Sept./Oct. 1995): 8.

17. Mark Reid, *Redefining Black Film* (Berkeley: University of California Press, 1993) p. 69.

18. Rustin, "The Reformation of a Rebel Without a Crew," p. 9.

19. Samuel Doria Medina, *La economía informal en Bolivia* (La Paz, 1986). Quoted in English in: Naomi Robbins, "Bolivia's Informal Economy," (Master's thesis, CUNY, 1990), 28.

20. George Yúdice, "Postmodernity and Transnational Capitalism" in *On Edge: The Crisis in Contemporary Latin American Culture*, eds. George Yúdice, Jean Franco and Juan Flores (Minneapolis: University of Minnesota Press, 1992), p. 2.

21. Ibid., p.9.

22. Ybarra-Frausto, "Interview," p. 208.

23. Ibid., p.214.

24. Interview with Robert Rodriguez for *Fresh Air*, National Public Radio in Philadelphia, September 6, 1995.

SELECT BIBLIOGRAPHY

Abarca, Onofre Antonio. "Viva la Onda Chicana: a Personal Perpective on Tex-Mex Music." *Forward: Journal of Socialist Thought* 8 (Spring 1988): 83-93.

Acuña, Rodolfo. *Occupied America: A History of Chicanos*. 3rd.ed. New York: Harper Collins Publishers, 1988.

Almaguer, Tomás. "Ideological Distortions in Recent Chicano Historiography: The Internal Model of Chicano Historical Interpretation." *Aztlán: A Journal of Chicano Studies* 18 (Spring 1981): 7-28.

_____. "Historical Notes on Chicano Oppression: The Dialectics of Racial and Class Domination in North America." *Aztlán: A Journal of Chicano Studies* 5 (Fall 1974): 27-54.

Anaya, Rudolfo A. and Francisco Lomelí, eds. *Aztlán: Essays on the Chicano Homeland*. Albuquerque: Academia/El Norte Publications, 1989.

Anzaldúa, Gloria. *Borderlands/La Frontera: The New Mestiza*. San Francisco: Spinsters/Aunt Lute, 1987.

Apte, Madhadev. *Humor and Laughter: An Anthropological Approach*. Ithaca: Cornell University Press, 1985.

Armas, José. "La Familia de la Raza." *De Colores: Journal of Chicano Expression and Thought* 3 (1976): 35-53.

Avalos, David and Brookman Phillip. *Café Mestizo (David Avalos)*. New York: INTAR, 1989.

Ayala Blanco, Jorge. "Artenstein y el Mito del Cine Chicano." *El Financiero*, 10 Sept. 1990, Cultural Sec., p. 71.

Barrera, Mario. "Story Structure in Latino Feature Films." In *Chicanos and Film: Essays on Chicano Representation and Resistance*, pp. 245-269. Edited by Chon Noriega. New York: Garland Publishing, 1991.

Barrios, Gregg. "Efraín Guiérrez y el nuevo cine chicano," *La Opinion*, 18 August, 1985, La Comunidad, p. 3.

_____. "A Cinema of Failure, A Cinema of Hunger: The Films of Efraín Gutiérrez." In *Chicano Cinema: Research, Reviews and Resources*, pp. 179-181. Edited by Gary Keller. Binghamton, N.Y.: Bilingual Review/Press, 1985.

Bhabha, Homi K. "The Other Question." *Screen* 24 (November/December 1983): 18-35.

Birri, Fernando. "For a Nationalist, Realist, Critical and Popular Cinema." *Screen* 26 (May/August 1985): 89-91.

Bobo, Jacqueline. "*The Color Purple*: Black Women as Cultural Readers," In *Female Spectators: Looking at Film and Television*, pp. 90-110. Edited by E. Deirdre Pribram. New York: Verso, 1988.

Bordwell, David; Staiger, Janet; and Thompson, Kristin. *The Classical Hollywood Cinema: Film Style and Mode of Production to 1960*. New York: Columbia University Press, 1985.

Brewer, J. Mason. *Humorous Folktales of the South Carolina Negro*. Orangeburg, S.C., 1945.

Brigham, J.C. "Ethnic Stereotypes." *Psychological Bulletin* 76 (Fall 1982): 15-38.

Buscombe, Edward. "The Idea of Genre in the American Cinema." *Screen* 11 (Fall 1979): 79-88.

Calderón, Hector and Saldívar, José David, eds. *Criticism in the Borderlands: Studies in Chicano Literature, Culture and Ideology*. Durham: N.C.: Duke University Press, 1991.

Camplís, Francisco X. "Towards the Development of a Raza Cinema." In *Perspectives on Chicano Education*, pp. 155-173. Edited by Tobias Gonzales and Sandra Gonzales. Stanford, California: Chicano Fellows/Stanford University, 1975; excerpted in *Tin Tan*, 2.5 (June 1977): 5-7; reprint ed., *Chicanos and Film: Essays on Chicano Representation and Resistance*, pp. 317-337. Edited by Chon Noriega. New York: Garland, 1991.

Candelaria, Cordelia. "Film Portrayals of La Mujer Hispana." *Agenda* 11 (May/June 1981): 32-36.

Cantú, Norma. "Women, Then and Now: An Analysis of the Adelita Image versus the Chicana Political Writer and Philosopher." In *Chicana Voices: Intersections of Class, Race and Gender*, pp. 8-11. Edited by Teresa Córdova et al. Austin: The Center for Mexican American Studies, 1986.

Carpentier, Alejo. *El siglo de las luces*. Caracas: Biblioteca Ayacucho, 1979.

Castañon García, Juan. "Bertolt Brecht and Luis Valdez: The Relation Between the Self and the Techniques in their Theatre." *De Colores: Journal of Chicano Expression and Thought* 5 (1980): 93-102.

Chabram, Angie. "Chicano Critical Discourse: An Emerging Cultural Practice." *Aztlán: A Journal of Chicano Studies* 18 (Fall 1987): 45-90.

Chanan, Michael. *Twenty-Five Years of New Latin American Cinema*. London: British Film Institue and Channel Four Television, 1983.

Chavez, Jennie V. "An Opinion: Women of the Mexican American Movement." *Mademoiselle*, April 1972, p. 82.

Chicano Art: Resistance and Affirmation. Los Angeles: UCLA Wight Art Gallery, 1990.

"Chicano Cinema Coalition Releases Statement on Boulevard Nights." *Chicano Cinema Newsletter* 1 (May 1979).

Citron, Michelle. "Women's Film Production: Going Mainstream." In *Female Spectators: Looking at Film and Television*, pp. 45-64. Edited by E. Deirdre Pribram. New York: Verso, 1988.

Cohen, Sandy. "Racial and Ethnic Humor in the United States," *Amerika Studien/American Studies* 30 (Fall 1985): 205-211.

Cook, William W. "Change the Joke and Slip the Yoke," *Journal of Ethnic Studies* 6 (Fall 1978): 98-121.

Cortés, Carlos. "Who is Maria? What is Juan? Dilemmas of Analyzing the Chicano Image in U.S. Feature Films," In *Chicanos and Film: Essays on Chicano Representation and Resistance*, pp. 83-105. Edited by Chon Noriega. New York: Garland Publishing, 1991.

Cripps, Thomas. *Slow Fade to Black*. Bloomington: Indiana University Press, 1978.

Cunniff, Tom. *People Weekly* 14, September 1987, p. 14.

Davis, Angela. *Women, Race and Class*. New York: Random House, 1981.

Dearborn, Mary. *Pocahontas' Daughters*. New York: Oxford University Press, 1986.

Del Castillo, Adelaida. "Malintzin Tenepal: A Preliminary Look into a New Perspective." In *Essays on La Mujer*, pp. 124-150. Edited by Rosaura Sanchez. Los Angeles: Chicano Studies Center Publications/University of California, Los Angeles, 1977.

Doane, Mary Ann. *The Desire to Desire: The Woman's Film of the 1940's*. Bloomington: Indiana University Press, 1987.

Documents of the Chicano Struggle. New York: Pathfinder Press, 1971.

Dubois, W.E.B. *The Souls of Black Folk*. New York: Signet, 1969.

Eagleton, Terry. "Marxism and the Past." *Salmagundi* 68/69 (Fall/Winter 1985-1986): 271-290.

Falkenberg, Pamela. "Hollywood and the Art Cinema as a Bipolar Modeling System." *Wide Angle* 7 (Fall 1988): 44-53.

Fields, Syd. *The Screenwriter's Workbook*. New York: Dell Trade Paperback, 1986.

Flores, Juan and George Yúdice. "Living Borders/Buscando America: Languages of Latino Self-formation." *Social Text: Theory/Culture/Ideology* 8 (1990): 57-84.

Ford, Paul L. *The New England Primer*. New York: Dodd, Mead, 1987.

Franco, Jean. "The Incorporation of Women: A Comparison of North American and Mexican Popular Narrative." In *Studies in Entertainment: Critical Approaches to Mass Culture*, pp. 119-138. Edited by Tania Modleski. Bloomington: Indiana University Press, 1986.

Fregoso, Rosa Linda. "Born in East L.A. and the Politics of Representation." *Cultural Studies* 4 (October 1990): 264-280.

_____. "Chicana Film Practices: Confronting the 'Many-Headed Demon of Oppression.'" In *Chicanos and Film: Essays on Chicano Representation and*

Resistance, pp. 189-205. Edited by Chon Noriega. New York: Garland Publishing, 1991.

———. *The Bronze Screen: Chicana and Chicano Film Culture.* Minneapolis: University of Minnestota Press, 1993.

Freud, Sigmund. *Jokes and Their Relation to the Unconsious.* Translated by James Strachey. New York: Penguin, 1960.

Friar, Natasha and Friar, Ralph. *The Only Good Indian.* New York: Drama Press, 1972.

Fried, Johathan, ed. *Guatemala in Rebellion.* New York: Grove Press, 1982.

Friedman, Jonathan. *Hollywood's Image of the Jew.* New York: Frederick Ungar, 1982.

———, ed. *Unspeakable Images: Ethnicity and the American Cinema.* Urbana: University of Illinois Press, 1991.

Fuentes, Victor. "Chicano Cinema: A Dialectic Between Voices and Images of the Autonomous Discourse Versus Those of the Dominant." In *Chicanos and Film: Essays on Chicano Representation and Resistance*, pp. 233-245. Edited by Chon Noriega. New York: Garland Publishing, 1991.

Fusco, Coco. "The Latino Boom in Hollywood." *Centro Bulletin* 8 (Spring): 31-36.

Gabriel, Teshome. *Third Cinema in the Third World: The Aesthetics of Liberation.* Ann Arbor: U.M.I. Research Press, 1982.

1990): 48-56.

———. "Theses on Memory and Identity: In Search of the Origin of the River Nile." *Emergences* 1: 130-137.

———. "Thoughts on Nomadic Aesthetics and the Black Independent Cinema: Traces of a Journey." In *Black Frames*, pp. 62-79. Edited by Mbye B. Cham and Claire Andrade-Watkins. Cambridge, Massachusetts: M.I.T. Press, 1988.

Gamboa, Harry Jr. "Silver Screening the Barrio." *Equal Opportunity Forum* 6 (November 1978): 6-7.

———. "Past imperfecto." In *Jump Cut: A Review of Contemporary Media* 39 (June, 1994): 93-95.

García, Mario T. "Mexican American Labor and the Left: The Association Nacional Mexico-Americana, 1949-1954." In *The Chicano Struggle: Analysis of Past and Present Efforts*, pp. 65-87. Edited by John Garcia, Theresa Córdova and Juan R. García. Binghamton N.Y.: Bilingual Press, 1984.

García, Juan Ramón. *Operation Wetback: The Mass Deportation of Mexican Undocumented Workers in 1954.* Westport, Conn.: Greenwood Press, 1980.

García Riera, Emilio. *Mexico Visto Por El Cine Extranjero.* 5 vols. Universidad de Guadalajara: Ediciones E.R.A., 1990.

García-Bahne, Betty. "La Chicana and the Chicano Family," In *Essays on La Mujer*, pp. 44-60. Edited by Rosaura Sanchez. Los Angeles: Chicano Studies Center Publications, 1977.

Garza, Hector. "A Directory of Chicano/Latino Films and Their Distributors." In *Chicano Cinema: Research, Reviews and Resources*, pp. 191-202. Edited by Gary Keller. Binghamton, N.Y.: Bilingual Press Review, 1985.

Gibson, Charles, ed. *The Black Legend: Anti-Spanish Attitudes in the Old and New World*. Durham, N.C.: Duke University Press, 1971.

Gittlin, Todd. *The Whole World Is Watching: Mass Media in the Making and Unmaking of the New Left*. Berkeley: University of California Press, 1980.

Gledhill, Christine. "The Melodramtic Field: An Investigation." In *Home is Where the Heart Is: Studies in Melodrama and the Woman's Film*, pp. 5-43. Edited by Christine Gledhill. London: B.F.I., 1987.

Goldman, Shifra and Ybarra-Frausto, Tomás. *Arte Chicano: A Comprehensive Annotated Bibliography of Chicano Art, 1965-1981*. Berkeley: University of California, Chicano Studies Library Publications Unit, 1985.

Gómez-Peña, Guillermo. "Border Culture and Deterritorialization." In *La Linea Quebrada Troupe No. 2*. San Diego: El Centro Cultural de la Raza, 1985.

_____. "Death on the Border: A Eulogy to Border Art." *High Performance* 14 (Spring, 1991): 8.

_____. "The Multicultural Paradigm." *High Performance* 12 (Fall 1989): 18-27.

Gómez-Peña, Guillermo and Kelley, Jeff, eds. *The Border Art Workshop: A Documentation of Five Years of Interdisciplinary Art Projects Dealing with U.S.-Mexico Border Issues, 1984-1989*. New York: Artists Space/La Jolla Museum of Contemporary Art, 1989.

Gonzáles, Rodolfo "Corky." "What Political Road for the Chicano Movement." *The Militant* (March 30, 1970); reprint ed., *A Documentary History of the Mexican Americans* p. 488. Edited by Wayne Moquin and Charles Van Doren. New York: Praeger Publishers, 1971.

González Navarro, Moises. *Población y Sociedad in México (1900-1970)*. Vol. 2. México: UNAM, 1974.

Gossett, Thomas F. *Race: The History of an Idea in America*. Dallas: S.M.U. Press, 1963.

Granjeda, Rafael. "The Pachuco in Chicano Poetry: The Process of Legend-Creation." *Revista Chicana-Riqueña* 7 (Otoño 1980): 45-60.

Gronk and Gamboa, Harry Jr. "The no-movie interview: Chicano art collective, Asco (1972-1987)." *Jump Cut: A Review of Contemporary Media* 39 (June, 1994): 91-92.

Gutiérrez, Felix F. and Schement, Jorge Reina. *Spanish Language Radio in the Southwestern United States*. Austin: The University of Texas Press, 1979.

Guitiérrez, José Angel. "The Chicano in Mexicano-Norte Americano Foreign Relations," In *Chicano-Mexicano Relations*, pp. 27-41. Edited by Tatcho Mindiola Jr. and Max Martinez. University Park: University of Houston Press, 1986.

Gutiérrez-Jones, Carl. "Legislating Languages: *The Ballad of Gregorio Cortez* and the *English Language Amendment.*" *The Americas Review* 17 (Summer 1989): 61-71.

Hadley-García, George. *Hispanic Hollywood: The Latins in Motions Pictures.* New York: Citadel Press, 1990.

Hanson, Cynthia. "The Hollywood Musical Biopic and the Regressive Performer." *Wide Angle* 10 (1988): 15-23.

Harasym, Sarah. *The Post-Colonial Critic: Interviews, Strategies, Dialogues.* New York: Routledge, 1990.

Hernandez, Guillermo. *Chicano Satire: A Study in Literary Culture.* Austin: University of Texas Press, 1991.

Hicks, Emily. "What the Broken Line is Not." *La Linea Quebrada/The Broken Line Troupe No. 2.* San Diego: El Centro Cultural de La Raza, 1985.

Hoffman, Abraham. *Unwanted Mexican-Americans in the Great Depression.* Tucson: University of Arizona Press, 1974.

Hooks, Bell. *Yearning.* Boston: Beacon Press, 1990.

Huaco-Nuzum, Carmen. "Despair in the barrio: AMERICAN ME." *Jump Cut: A Review of Contemporary Media* 38 (June, 1993): 92-95.

Huerta, Jorge. *Chicano Theatre: Themes and Forms.* Ypsilanti, Michigan: Bilingual Press/Editorial Bilingue, 1982.

Johansen, Jason C. "Pensamientos: Notes on Chicano Cinema," *Chicano Cinema Newsletter* 1 (June 1979): 6-8; reprinted ed., *Jump Cut* 23 (October 1980): 9-10; and reprint ed., *Chicanos and Film: Essays on Chicano Representation and Resistance*, pp. 337-341. Edited by Chon Noriega. New York: Garland Publishing, 1991.

Johnson, Kenneth F. *Mexican Democracy: A Critical View.* New York: Praeger, 1978.

Keller, Gary. "The Image of the Chicano in Mexican, United States and Chicano Cinema: An Overview." In *Chicano Cinema: Research, Reviews and Resources*4, pp. 13-58. Edited by Gary Keller. Binghamton, N.Y.: Bilingual Review Press, 1985.

Klor de Alva, J. Jorge. "Aztlán, Boriquen and Hispanic Nationalism in the United States." In *Aztlán: Essays on the Chicano Homeland*, pp. 135-172. Edited by Rudolfo Anaya and Francisco Lomelí. Albuquerque: Academia/El Norte Publications, 1989.

Kuhn, Annette. *Women's Pictures.* London: Routledge and Kegan Paul, 1982.

Lamb, Blaine P. "The Convenient Villain: The Early Cinema Views of the Mexican-American." *Journal of the West* 14 (October 1975): 75-81.

Lattin, Vernon, ed. *Contemporary Chicano Fiction: A Critical Survey.* Binghamton, N.Y.: Bilingual Press/Editorial Bilingue, 1986.

Leab, Daniel. *From Sambo to Superspade.* Boston: Houghton Mifflin Co., 1975.

Leal, Luis. "In Search of Aztlán." *Denver Quarterly* 16 (Fall 1981): pp. 6-24.

Levine, Lawrence W. *Black Culture and Black Consciousness*. New York: Oxford University Press, 1977.

Lewels, Francisco J., Jr. *The Uses of the Media by the Chicano Movement: A Study of Minority Access*. New York: Praeger Publishers, 1974.

Limón, José. "Stereotyping and Chicano Resistance: An Historical Dimension." *Aztlán: An International Journal of Chicano Studies Research* 4 (Fall 1973): 257-270.

Linfield, Susan. "Close Up: Luis Valdez." *American Film* (July/August 1987): p.15.

List, Christine. "A Latino/a Politics of Language: BREAK OF DAWN." *Jump Cut: A Review of Contemporary Media* 38 (June, 1993): 81-86.

_____. "EL NORTE: Ideology and Immigration." *Jump Cut: A Review of Contemporary Media* 34 (1989): 27-31.

_____. "Self-Directed Stereotyping in the Films of Cheech Marin." In *Chicanos and Film*, pp. 183-194. Edited by Chon Noriega. New York: Garland Publishing, 1992.

López, Sonia A. "The Role of the Chicana within the Student Movement." In *Essays on La Mujer*, pp. 16-29. Edited by Rosaura Sanchez. Los Angeles: University of California Press, 1977.

López, Ana. "An 'Other' History: The New Latin American Cinema." *Radical History Review* 42 (1988): 93-116.

_____. "Are All Latins from Manhattan: Hollywood Ethnography and Cultural Colonialism." In *Unspeakable Images: Ethnicity and the American Cinema*, pp. 404-424. Edited by Lester Friedman. Urbana: University of Illinois, 1991.

_____. "The Melodrama in Latin America: Films, Telenovelas and the Currency of a Popular Form." *Wideangle* 7 (Fall 1988): 5-13.

Lubenow, Gerald C. "Putting the Border Onstage," *Newsweek*, 4 May, 1987, p. 79.

McLean, Adrienne. "I'm a Casino: Transformation, Ethnicity and Authenticity in the Construction of Rita Hayworth, American Love Goddess." *Journal of Film and Video* 44.3-4 (Fall-Winter 1992-93): 8-24

Maciel, David. *El Norte: The U.S.-Mexican Border in Contemporary Cinema*. San Diego: Institute for Regional Studies of the Californias, San Diego State University, 1990.

Marcuse, Herbert. *A Critique of Pure Tolerance*. Boston: Beacon Press, 1969.

Martín-Barbero, Jesús. "Communication from Culture: The Crisis of the National and the Emergence of the Popular." *Media, Culture and Society* 10 (1988): 447-465.

_____. "Retos a la investigación de comunicación en América Latina." *Revista ININCO* 2 (Caracas), 1981.

Mazón, Mauricio. *The Zoot-Suit Riots: The Psychology of Symbolic Annihilation*. Austin: University of Texas Press, 1984.

Meier, Matt S. and Rivera, Feliciano. *The Chicanos: A History of Mexican Americans*. New York: Hill and Wang, 1972.

Menchú, Rigoberta. *I Rigoberta Menchú: An Indian Woman in Guatemala*. London: Verso, 1984.

Mercer, Kobena. "Diaspora Culture and the Dialogic Imagination: The Aesthetics of Black Independent Film in Britain." In *Black Frames*, pp. 50-61. Edited by Mbye B. Cham and Claire Andrade-Watkins. Cambridge, Massachusetts: M.I.T. Press, 1988.

Middleton, Russell and Moland, James. "Humor in Negro and White Subcultures." *American Sociological Review* 24 (1959): 53-70.

_____. "Negro and White Reactions to Racial Humor." *Sociometry* 23 (Fall 1973): 171-190.

Minh-ha, Trinh T. *Woman, Native, Other*. Berkeley: University of California Press, 1989.

Modleski, Tania. "Time and Desire in the Woman's Film." *Cinema Journal* 23 (Spring 1984): 26-27.

Monsivaís, Carlos. "The Culture of the Frontier: The Mexican Side." In *Views from Across the Border: The United States and Mexico*, pp. 50-67. Edited by Stanley Ross. Albuquerque: University of New Mexico, 1978.

Montaño, Teresa and Dennis Vigil. "English-only: Right Wing's Power of Babble." *Forward: A Journal of Socialist Thought* 8 (Spring 1988): 51-83.

Mora, Carl J. *Mexican Cinema: Reflections of a Society, 1986-1980*. Berkeley: University of California Press, 1982.

Morgan, Patricia. *Shame of a Nation: A Documented Story of Police-State Terror Against Mexican Americans in the U.S.A.* Los Angeles: Los Angeles Committee for Protection of the Foreign Born, 1954.

Muñoz, Carlos Jr. *Youth, Identity, Power: The Chicano Movement*. New York: Verso, 1989.

Muwakkil, Salim. "Spike Lee and the Image Police." *Cineaste* 7, (April 1990): 35-36.

Navarro, Armando. "The Evolution of Chicano Politics" *Aztlán: A Journal of Chicano Studies* 5 (Fall 1972): 57-84.

Neale, Stephen. *Genre*. London: British Film Institute, 1980.

Nichols, Bill. *Ideology and the Image: Social Presentation in the Cinema and Other Media*. Bloomington: Indiana University Press, 1981.

Noriega, Chon. "Café Oralé: Narrative Structure in *Born in East L.A. Tonantzin* 8 (February 1991): 17-18.

_____. "Citizen Chicano: The Trials and Titillations of Ethnicity in the American Cinema, 1935 - 1962." *Social Research* 58 (Summer 1991): 412-438.

_____, ed. *Chicanos and Film: Essays on Chicano Representation and Resistance*. New York: Garland Publishing, 1991. Also in paperback with University of Minnesota Press, 1992.

_____. "Road to Aztlán: Chicanos and Narrative Cinema." Ph.D. dissertation, Stanford University, 1991.

_____. "The Aesthetic Discourse: Reading Chicano Cinema Since *La Bamba.*" *Centro Bulletin* 3 (Winter 1990-1991): 55-71.

_____. "The Numbers Game." *Jump Cut: A Review of Contemporary Media* 39 (June 1994): 107-111.

Oring, Edward. "Everything is a Shade of Elephant: An Alternative to a Psychoanalysis of Humor." *New York Folklore* (Fall 1973): 149-159.

Oroña-Córdova, Roberta. "*Zoot Suit* and the *Pachuco* Phenomenon: An Interview with Luis Valdez." *Revista Chicano-Riquena* 11 (1983): 95-110.

Oshana, Mayann. *Women of color: A Filmography of Minority and Third World Women.* New York: Garland, 1985.

Padilla, Felix. *Latino Ethnic Consciousness: The Case of Mexican Americans and Puerto Ricans in Chicago.* Notre Dame: University of Notre Dame Press, 1985.

Padilla, Genero. "Myth and Comparative Cultural Nationalism: The Ideological Uses of Aztlán." In *Aztlán: Essays of the Chicano Homeland*, pp. 111-135. Edited by Rudolfo Anaya and Francisco Lomelí. Albuquerque: Academia/El Norte Press, 1989.

Paredes, Américo. "Folk Medicine and Intercultural Jest," In *Spanish Speaking People in the United States: Proceedings of the 1968 Annual Spring Meeting of the American Ethnological Society*, pp. 104-199. Edited by June Helm. Seattle: University of Washington Press, 1968.

Paredes, Américo. *With Pistol in Hand: A Border Ballad and Its Hero.* Austin: University of Texas Press, 1971.

Paredes, Raymund A. "Origins of Anti-Mexican Sentiment in the United States," In *New Directions in Chicano Scholarship*, pp. 139-165. Edited by Ricardo Romo and Raymund Paredes. La Jolla, California: University of California Press, 1978.

Paz, Octavio. *The Labyrinth of Solitude, Life and Thought in Mexico.* Translated by Lysander Kemp. New York: Grove Press, 1962.

"Pensamientos: Latinos and CPB, In Quest of National Programming." *Chicano Cinema Newsletter* 1 (August 1979).

Pettit, Arthur. *Images of the Mexican American in Fiction and Film.* College Station, Texas: Texas A&M University Press, 1980.

Pina, Michael. "The Archaic, Historical and Mythicized Dimensions of Aztlán." In *Aztlán: Essays on the Chicano Homeland*, pp. 14-49. Edited by Rudolfo Anaya and Francisco Lomelí. Albuquerque: Academia/El Norte Publications, 1989.

Plascencia, Luis F.B. "Lowriding in the Southwest." In *History Culture and Society: Chicano Studies in the 1980's*, pp. 145-167. Edited by the National Association for Chicano Studies. Ypsilanti, Michigan: Bilingual Press/Editorial Bilingue, 1983.

Porath, Don. "Chicanos and Existentialism." *De Colores: Journal of Chicano Expression and Thought* 1 (Spring 1974): 6-29.

Prida, Dolores. "*El Norte*: A Landmark Latino Film." *Nuestro*, May, 1984, pp. 49-51.

Puig, Claudia. "Latino Writers Form Group to Fight Stereotypes." *Los Angeles Times*, 10 August, 1989, sec. 4, p. 9.

Ramírez Berg, Charles. *Cinema of Solitude: A Critical Study of Mexican Film*. Austin: University of Texas Press, 1992.

_____. "Images and Counterimages of the Hispanic in Hollywood." *Tonantzin* 6 (November 1988): 12-13.

_____. "Stereotyping in Films in General and of the Hispanic in Particular." *The Howard Journal of Communications* 2 (Summer 1990): 286-300.

_____. "Y basta con la Hollywood paradigm! Strategies for Latino screenwriters." *Jump Cut: A Review of Contemporary Media* 38 (June, 1993): 96-104.

Reid, Mark A. *Redefining Black Film*. Berkeley: University of California Press, 1993

Reyes, Luis and Rubie, Peter. *Hispanics in Hollywood: An Encyclopedia of Film and Television*. New York: Garland Publishing, 1994.

Reyna, José. "Contemporary Myths in Chicano Joke Tradition." In *Renato Rosaldo Lecture Series 3: 1985-1986*, pp. . Edited by Ignacio García. Tucson: Arizona Board of Regents, 1987.

Robertson, William. *The History of America*. New York: J. Harper, 1977.

Rodriguez, Robert. *Rebel Without a Crew: Or How a 23-Year-Old Filmmaker with $7000 Became a Hollywood Player*. New York: Penguin, 1995.

Roeder, George H., Jr. "Mexicans in the Movies: The Image of Mexicans in American Films, 1894-1947." Ph.D. dissertation, University of Wisconsin, 1971.

Romo, Ricardo and Paredes, Raymund, eds. *New Directions in Chicano Scholarship*. La Jolla, California: University of California Press, 1978.

Rosen, David. *Off Hollywood: The Making and Marketing of Independent Films*. New York: Grove Weidenfeld, 1990.

Saalfield, Catherine and Ray Navarro. "Not Just Back and White: AIDS Media and People of Color." *Centro Bulletin* 2 (Spring 1990): 70 -79.

Said, Edward. *Orientalism*. New York: Vintage Books, 1979.

Saldívar, José David. *The Dialectics of Our America: Geneology, Cultural Critique, and Literary History*. Durham: Duke University Press, 1990.

Saldívar, Ramón. *Chicano Narrative: The Dialectics of Difference*. Madison: University of Wisconsin Press, 1990.

Samora, Julian. "Mexican Immigration," In *Introduction to Chicano Studies*, pp. 81-82. Edited by Livie Isauro Duran and H. Russell Bernard. New York: Macmillan Publishing Co., Inc. 1982.

Sanchez, Juan Carlos. "Nacido al Este de Los Angeles." *Cine Cubano* 121 (1988): 81-82.

Sánchez, Rosaura. "Postmodernism and Chicano Literature." *Aztlán: A Journal of Chicano Studies* 18 (Fall 1987): 1-14.

Sánchez-Tranquilino, Marcos and John Tagg. "The Pachuco's Flayed Hide: The Museum, Identity and Buenas Garras." Paper presented at the Cultural Studies Conference, University of Illinois at Urbana, 5 April 1990.

Shohat, Ella and Stam, Robert. *Unthinking Eurocentrism: Multiculturalism and the Media.* New York: Routledge, 1994.

Sobchack, Vivian. "Postmodern Modes of Ethnicity." In *Unspeakable Images: Ethnicity and American Cinema*, pp. 329-352. Edited by Lester Friedman. Urbana: University of Illinois Press, 1991.

Sommers, Joseph and Tomás Ybarra-Frausto, eds. *Modern Chicano Writers: A Collection of Critical Essays.* Englewood Cliffs, N.J.: Prentice-Hall, 1979.

Springer, Claudia. "Comprehension and Crisis: Reporter Films and the Third World." In *Unspeakable Images: Ethnicity and the American Cinema*, pp. 167-190. Edited by Lester Friedman. Urbana: University of Illinois Press, 1991.

Louise Spence and Robert Stam. "Colonialism, Racism and Representation." In *Movies and Methods*, pp. 632-649. Edited by Bill Nichols. Berkeley: University of California Press, 1985.

Robert Stam. "Bakhtin, Polyphony, and Ethnic/Racial Representation." In *Unspeakable Images: Ethnicity and the American Cinema*, pp. 251-177. Edited by Lester Friedman. Urbana: University of Illinois Press, 1991.

"Statement of Purpose." *Chicano Cinema Newsletter* 1 (February 1979): 8.

Studlar, Gaylyn and David Desser. "Never Having to Say You're Sorry: Rambo's Rewriting of the Vietnam War." *Film Quarterly* 42 (1988): 9-16.

Taylor, Clyde. "WE DON'T NEED ANOTHER HERO: Anti-Theses on Aesthetics," In *Blackframes*, pp. 80-85. Edited by Mbye B. Cham and Claire Andrade-Watkins. Cambridge, Massachusetts: M.I.T. Press, 1988.

Taylor, Ronald B. *Chavez and the Farm Workers.* Boston: Beacon Press, 1975.

Treviño, Jesús Salvador. "Chicano Cinema." *New Scholar* 8 (1982): 167-180.

Valdez, Luis and El Teatro Campesino. *Actos.* San Juan Bautista, California: Cucaracha Publications, 1971.

Valle, Victor. "A Chicano Reporter in 'Hispanic Hollywood': Editorial Agendas and the Culture of Professional Journalism." In *Chicanos and Film: Essays on Chicano Representation and Resistance*, pp. 291-307. Edited by Chon Noriega. New York: Garland Publishing, 1991.

Vargas, Lucila. "El Norte." *The Americas Review* 14 (Spring 1986): 89-91.

Vasconcelos, José. "The Race Problem in Latin America," In *Introduction to Chicano Studies*, pp. 5-27. Edited by Livie Duran and H.R. Bernard. New York: Macmillan, 1973.

Wallace, Michelle. *Black Macho and the Myth of the Superwoman.* New York: Dell Press, 1987.

West, Cornel. "Diverse New World." *Democratic Left* 19 (July/August 1991): 7-12.

West, Dennis and Crowdus, Gary. "Cheech Cleans Up His Act." *Cineaste* 16 (July 1988): 34-37.

Williams, Linda. "Type and Stereotype: Chicana Images in Film." In *Chicano Cinema: Research, Reviews and Resources*, pp. 94-107. Edited by Gary Keller. Binghamton, N.Y.: Bilingual Review/Press, 1985.

Woll, Allen L. *The Latin Image in American Film.* Los Angeles: University of California Press, 1977.

_____. and Miller, Randall. *Ethnic and Racial Images in American Film and Television.* New York: Garland, 1987.

Yúdice, George, Franco, Jean and Flores, Juan. *On Edge: The Crisis of Contemporary Latin American Culture.* Minneapolis: University of Minnesota Press, 1992.

INDEX

177